THE

ESTᴰ 1742

WHITBREAD
BOOK OF
SCOUSEOLOGY

by
PHIL YOUNG and JIM BELLEW

supported by the
LIVERPOOL ECHO

"AN ANTHOLOGY OF MERSEYSIDE"

THE WHITBREAD BOOK
OF SCOUSEOLOGY

ISBN 0 9509801 3 7

Published by
Brunswick Printing and Publishing Co. Ltd.
Gibraltar Row, Liverpool L3 7HJ
and
Scouse Promotions Ltd.

Design and typesetting by Coleman Print Services Ltd., Liverpool.
Printed by Printfine Ltd., Liverpool.

The authors wish to thank:

Arthur Johnson of the Liverpool Echo for his help, support and
enthusiasm.

Colin Hunt of the Liverpool Echo for his assistance in validating,
indexing and invaluable help with the illustrations.

Peter Hobbs and Tony Garforth of Whitbread (Merseyside) Ltd.
Alan Cameron of MCC P.R. Ltd. Altrincham.

Steve and Alan Coleman and Ossie Jones of Coleman Print Services.

Michael Foot for permission to reproduce his poem in full.

THE AUTHORS

BELLEW YOUNG
by Young by Bellew

Bellew was born in Liverpool but I'm unable to establish when. He tells me his records were destroyed soon after his birth. He was educated, loosely speaking, at Holy Name and Walton Tech. He played in goal for Holy Name and was nicknamed "The Cat", either because he gave the rest of the defence kittens or he needed nine lives as a result of threats made by Holy Name supporters. His career has included spells at Connolly's, Dunlop's, the Merchant Navy, Prestcold, all of which were fairly undistinguished (thats what it said on the references anyway). A chance remark that he looked good in a suit prompted him to try Management and an American company gave him a suitcase and flew him all over the world. He's the only person I know whose passport comes in chapters. He returned to Blighty (if that doesn't give his age away nothing does) and became the MD of a group of companies. He is a Fellow of the Institute of Directors but was disappointed to learn that they don't run a works football team. As a former goalkeeper (he used to play for the Hamlet) he lists among his heroes Cyril Sidlow, Charlie Ashcroft, Tommy Younger, Ray Clemence and Bruce of course.
He tells me there is nothing he likes better to settle down and have a good read of the Echo while enjoying a pint or two of Whitbread's Trophy bitter.
He's always been a crawler.

Young was born at 57 Adelaide Road, Liverpool 7. There is no plaque and as far as can be ascertained subsequent occupiers have never been bothered by sightseers. He attended Rathbone Primary School Edge Hill until his parents successful lobbying of the Housing Department secured a "detached bungalow" on the Belle Vale pre-fab estate. After attending Gateacre Primary, Joseph Williams and Holt school's Young decided, on getting a job as an office boy, to settle for a career in commerce. His jobs included every type of clerk except Clerk of Works, every kind of salesman except the one that wins the prizes, Postal and Telegraph officer, progress chaser . . . In the 1970's he managed a branch office of Sykes Waterhouse & Co before leaving to do missionary work in Buckinghamshire. He worked in Aylesbury and the City of London and managed two branches of Provincial Building Society in Birmingham. Young maintains he was in the same class as Paul McCartney. I was prepared to argue until I realised he meant at school. It now appears he reckons he's five years younger than Paul.
His most memorable moment? Playing Widow Twankey in pantomime in 1981.
His most disappointing moment? Not being asked to play Widow Twankey in 1982.
He's now returned to Merseyside and we've started a new company, Scouse Promotions Ltd.

FOREWORD

In these days of the trivia craze, when the utmost pleasure is realised from knowing more of those irritating titbits than the next man, how can yet another trivia book create excitement? — (answer) — When it's a trivia book about our own hometown — Liverpool.

You now have in your hand the ultimate argument settler, the bible of Scouse facts. No more will you be thwarted by the bar-room bore who knows everything. With this volume you have the ammunition to fight back with a priceless compendium of catalogued curios about our hometown. What is Ian Botham's connection with Merseyside? What does the series 'Brideshead Revisited' have Liverpool to thank for? Where was Peter Adamson really born? Yet the A-Z of Scouseology isn't just a massive list of facts. It's put together with the humour and the asides Scousers are noted for and the authors have obviously enjoyed every moment of their research into the depths of Scouse trivia, and that shines through.

So be ready for an outbreak of Scouse trivia in pubs, clubs, and restaurants. Expect to be asked such riveting posers as which Liverpool-born assassin was apprehended by Bamber Gascoigne? What does Smithdown Road Hospital have to do with a world-famous sex change? Where was Arthur Askey born? Who played in goal for the Back Entry Diddlers? All this and more is revealed within. Cherish this volume, it could be the first of many volumes destined to keep Scouse knowledge seekers locked in the loo for an eternity!

BILLY BUTLER

AUTHORS' DEDICATIONS
To the people, places and events of Liverpool and Merseyside, but especially to:

Kitty Draycot and the Bridgefield Road Coronation party of 1953. "Colonel" Close and his lady, Little Jimmy from Pegrams, Tommy the Print, the Mediterranean Lounge at the Bradford, Fred Jackson and Tony Connor, "Tich" Percival (who was chosen to plant the Coronation tree), "Pop", Gore, "Pop" Wallard, Miss Breeze and Miss Ward, Harry Grenoble, Mrs. Earle at Cloverdale Road Co-op (149200). The Last Lads from Dunlops Walton, the Masque Coffee Bar, 'Sadie' from the Old Royal, Felix the Cat, the Crosville overcoat, Scott's Mobile shop, Pete 'that'll do me" Hartley, Harry Denison (congratulations on 25 years), Mrs. Windsor from the Cabin, Bunney's toy shop, Kay Kennedy (where are you now?) Hilary from the Airport and the missing missive, Norman Castle, Wally and his Fats Waller impersonations, Ha-Ha Robertson, Deritage and Hodge, Mrs. Orr and the Aunts, Jimmy Adamson and the Fusegear office tontine 1964, Matty Joyce in the Stores, Billy Ellis at the piano, the bench at Connolly's, Mrs. Johnson (perhaps Liverpool's first lady football coach whose son played for Everton AND Liverpool), Bellew's pantry and the armadillo's, a Vauxhall Viva HGY 590C, Pat and Susie, Pete Cartin (you remember Harry Hardy!), Johnnie Hilton and his orchestra, Tony Meredith and "St. Phil's", Big Eggo from the Copplehouse, Johnny McGowan, Mrs. Close and Alan, Brenda Kerr and June Stalker, Madeline, Flo, Barbara and Eve (those lovely corned beef butties) Mr. and Mrs. Harris and those parties at 57. Pam (of the three surnames) Joe's Café in Duke Street, the Mardi Gras, the Latin Quarter, the Bishopgate Street air-raid shelter, Johnnie Ray in the Legs of Man. Mr. Fallon and Geoff, Pat Bamford, Anne and Kenny Owens, the Spanish House, El Cabala, Bold Street, the Blue Ball, Prescot Street, the Chanticleer, Mr. Chaudray at the Kismet, Norman 'Nat King Cole' Clephon, Sonny, Keith and Mr. and Mrs. Puckey, Marilyn and Uncle Sid, Harry Zambia, Grollo, Teddy Fish, the 'Wolf', the 'Dancing Bear', Toddy and the imaginary washing line, Cathy at the Echo, "Tucker" Weaver and his unique bowling action, Billy Moorcroft and Smith Gorrie and Young who held out successfully in the 1957 Final at Anfield, Nurse Pat Pollock, the Porthole, the Beachcomber, two Bill Naylors, Cooper's in Church Street, Mr. Hunt from Bennett Hill's (what a cruise) Brian Fagin and the FS Appreciation Society at the Swan, London Road, Billy Martins, Swainsons, Thompsons and Ossie Wades, the Harlequin, the White City croupiers, 1966. Pete the Cartoonist, shorthand typists from West Derby who were Johnny Mathis fans, McCann the Barnsley winger who scored "New footy's" greatest goal, Pete Robbo and that silver streak, Moira, Frances Fenlon, Arthur Dickinson, Charlie Flynn, Lillian, John Seel, Brian "the Guardsman" Rainford, Irene Brown, the late great Ray Backhouse, the white £5 note at Yates' Wine Lodge, Robin Ashurst, "Dai" Morgan and "Dai" Brew, Alan Turner (born 19 February, 1942), Mrs. Hunt, Netta and the tea leaves, Eileen from Bootle and Derek from Southport. The Jokers Club, "so this is the swinging city", The Peking, London Road, the Cathay, Caroline Sartori, Harry Lightcake, those in the Lee Park Hotel when we heard of Kennedy's assassination, Billy (Liverpool 5-Spurs 2) Draycot, Hilda Starley and Ella, Joey Kennedy, Leo on the piano at the Endbutt, Ryan's Bistro, Danny, Harold,

Willie, Chrissie, Philly and Jimmy at the Shaftesbury reunion, 'Pop' Haworth of the Sally Army, Mr. Lochead and "Come in, Mrs. Marshall", Ernie Conning (back from Down Under) John Crosby at Jaycee's, Waldeis Weekes and Wilmington, and also Levy and Robinson who missed those Holt assemblies, Mr. Boardman, Ricky, Brian and Doreen (all Gilbertsons but not knowingly related), Chicken Vindaloo, (at 4 a.m.), Dave Schlechte (still spelling his name correctly), Derek 'Catalogue' Hill and his 2IC, Andy Kirk, Malcolm Derrick, Muriel Jones, Barbara Jones, Harry "I like cold custard, Don" Jones, Norman Jones, Roy Jones (ever tried keeping up with them?) Flo Bellew, Lil' Roberts, Nellie Tomlinson's retirement party, the fella that carried the board around Anfield, Goodison and the Stadium, the Royal Tiger, Pat Burns, Frank Caton, Effin Nelly's, the Temple, the Peppermint Lounge, the New Coliseum cinema, the Capital Cinema, Overton Street, the Rex (Vera Ellen), Mary Williams (a Juliet Prowse lookalike), Orrell Park Pleasure Ground (pleasure ground?), homemade tomato soup and Pommes Bellew, Pete Kearney, a letter to Bill before the Ajax return match (to no avail), Wagon and Trailer, Colette, the Stork Hotel, Miss England 1959, Bill Buckle, Bobby Wilson, Mrs. Wilson at the piano, Jimmy Swords, Dan English, Marilyn and Paul, Sturla's cheques, the Co-op divvy, Bobby Jameson (what a goalie!) Geoff and Gag Kerr, the Doc, halves of Bass at the Angel. Philly Walker, Linda Benn and Gaynor Lacey, Pete Price (chef, croupier and comedian) the Pinewoods pub when Liverpool won in Rome, DMM, Ray ACA and Sue, Dowthers of the Fifth, Freddie Corbett and his band, Reece's, the Locarno, the Karonga Road Coronation party 1953, Bert Cook — one of Liverpool's great comedians, the West Derby Village Hall, the 1986 President of Waterloo RUFC and his missus Sheila (deadly with the blue lavatory cleaner) Bill Cliffe at Everton Supporters' Club, Wally Vann, Stan Shacklady, the "mysterious" John Clarke, Shy Tot, the overturned "Australian" on Queens Drive, Smoke Bellew, Darquell (at 33-1), Golden Mean (at 28-1), the new Golden Phoenix (the Vaughans were there too) mustard on cheese, Mr. Parry, Clarkey, songs from the shows, a fancy dress party in Chelwood Avenue in 1969, Flossie, Stan from the TA. Blackler's grotto, the Cabaret Club, Jimmy Tansey (and that Jackie Milburn "dragback" at Goodison) the Majestic cinema Ron Begley, St. Stephen's, Gateacre, Our Lady of the Assumption, Kenny Smythe, Julie and Carol Arthur, Mr. Prickett the milkman, a Ford Anglia that never, never started. Gordon and Ronnie, Jim Folger, George Quirk, Paul McCartney ("No thanks, Paul, I don't want to join your group"), Pat Murphy, Stan Cato, Harry Webb (no, not Cliff), Pete Willo (of the mohair suits) Pete Browne, the Festival of Britain firework display 1951), charas to the lights, Butterfields, lots of liverine, Aunty Ivy, Cathy and Terry, Carol and Dave, Tony and Rene, Elaine now at Newcastle University, Ricky and Marcello, Frank, several Father Kellys, the Gilmours (lovely Kippers from the IoM), Jean (now in deepest Devon), John Kemp, Barbara at the Spiral Staircase, Pauline Ferns, the chandler's at the corner of the street, Mums and Dads and finally . . . **Linda, Danielle Samantha, Nicholas James and Kathryn Elizabeth.**

‘In the town where I was born . . .

ABERCROMBIE, Lascelles
Was a lecturer in poetry at Liverpool University and a journalist in Liverpool. Produced critical essay on Thomas Hardy (1912), a collection of poems "Interludes and Poems" and the play "The Sale of St. Thomas".

ABRAHAM, Cyril
Spent thirteen years in the Merchant Navy after serving his apprenticeship with the Liverpool shipping line of Lamport and Holt. No doubt he was gathering information for the highly successful BBC TV series he created in the early 1970's "The Onedin Line". The series, a world-wide hit, was set in nineteenth century Liverpool and based around the ship-owning Onedin family.

ADAMSON, Peter
Liverpool actor who was in the original cast of Granada TV's "Coronation Street" when it first came to the screen in December 1960. He had made the character he played, Len

Fairclough, a household name long before he was written out of the series in 1983. A family dispute exists about his birth-place. It was in Molyneux Road, Wavertree and, Peter maintains, in a fish and chip shop. However, other members of the family, whilst agreeing he was a chip off the old block, do not fully agree on the exact nature of the usage of his birth-plaice.

ADELPHI The
The most famous of Liverpool hotels, a sumptuous extravagant place in its heyday. Far beyond the economic reach of the average Liverpudlian and confirmed by the bus conductor who when asked by a potential passenger "Do you stop at the Adelphi?" replied "What! On my wages, you must be joking".
The original Adelphi, described by Dickens as the best in the world, has gone, but the replacement, much to commend in modern architectural terms, was designed internally to emulate the luxurious ocean going liners of the transatlantic era. Having recently been restored to its former glory, was used for scenes depicting an Atlantic liner crossing in the Granada TV masterpiece "Brideshead Revisited".

AIGBURTH
Suburb of Liverpool, original venue of Liverpool RUFC and a cricket ground located on the banks of the Mersey. Lancashire have played many county games there over the

years and, in a match against the Australian tourists, Ted MacDonald bowled Don Bradman before the great man had reached double figures. The first bowler in English first class cricket to be no-balled for throwing occurred at the ground in July 1885 when George Jowett from Roby, Huyton, was called, playing for Lancashire against Surrey. Lancashire's best opening stand was made at Aigburth, 368 by Archie MacLaren and R. H. Spooner in 1903 v. Gloucestershire. In a special 'Roses' match in July 1913, to celebrate George V's visit to the City, Harry Dean took 17 for 91 for Lancs. against Yorkshire, the county's best match figures.

Aigburth's traditionally 'green' wicket was well illustrated on 15th May, 1924, when Glamorgan were bowled out for 22. Lancashire had done little better having been dismissed for 49 in their first innings.

Among Aigburth's notable residents over the years was Sir William Watson (1858-1935), the poet.

AINTREE

World-famous suburb of Liverpool as venue for the world's greatest steeplechase, the Grand National. Run each spring over 4 miles 856 yards, the race attracts world-wide interest and has produced some of racing's most dramatic memories. The 1956 National when the Queen Mother's horse Devon Loch had only to stay on its feet to win, when suddenly, inexplicably, it fell, believing it was jumping a fence that wasn't there, and Dave Dick rode E.S.B. to victory. Devon Loch's jockey, Dick Francis, now a best-selling thriller writer, maintained that the roar of the crowd had startled the horse. In 1981, cancer victim Bob Champion riding a horse that had been written off, Aldaniti, was first past the post. And the

Ikin and Dyson batting for Lancashire against Middlesex and taking a run off fast bowler Moss in 1955.

John Buckingham and Foinavon are led back in triumph.

greatest Aintree hero of them all, "Rummy" who captured the nation's hearts in the 1970's with his three victories. And do you know anyone who backed 100-1 winner Foinavon in one of the most sensational races ever in 1967? The motor-racing circuit was one of the best and fastest in Britain and was the scene of five British Grand Prix between 1955-62. Stirling Moss won in 1955 and 1957, Brabham in 1959, Von Tripps in 1961 and Jim Clark in 1962.

Albert Dock

3

**ALBERT
DOCK
VILLAGE**

The largest collection of Grade One Listed Buildings in Britain, originally designed by Jesse Hartley and opened by Prince Albert in 1846. The 'village' incorporates specialist shops, pubs, restaurants, offices and apartments in a stunning marina-style setting.

The magnificent Maritime Museum, incorporating an imaginative re-creation of Liverpool's 19th century dockland — when millions of emigrants passed through on their way to the new world — is also located here. The Northern Tate Gallery of Modern Art is due to open in 1988.

The 'village' is already an exciting tourist attraction and, when completed, it will form the first stage of the most spectacular waterfront regeneration in Europe.

Europe's most prestigious award for architectural conservation was won in 1986 by the Merseyside Development Corporation for its restoration of the Dock complex.

ALEXANDER, Jean

The Liverpool actress's brilliant portrayal of Hilda Ogden in Granada TV's "Coronation Street" has long been one of the programme's best attractions. Jean projects the character's interferring gossipy personality to perfection, and still manages to win our sympathy and understanding for her frailties.

ALMOND, Blessed John

Born in Allerton in 1577 and educated mainly in Ireland, he studied at the English College in Rome and in 1601 was ordained a priest. He spent time in Newgate and Gatehouse gaols and was eventually accused and convicted of being a Catholic priest and executed at Tyburn in 1612. He was canonized by Pope Paul VI in 1970 and his feast day is 25th October.

ALTON, David Patrick

MP for Mossley Hill. Educated in Liverpool, he became one of Britain's youngest City Councillors in 1972 when he was 21, and later youngest MP and Chief Whip.

ALTWEGG, Jeanette

Liverpool-born ice skater, who won an Olympic gold medal at Oslo in 1952. She was World Champion in 1951 and in the following year retained her title as well as winning the inaugural Sportswoman of the Year award. She also won a bronze medal in the 1948 Winter Olympics in St. Moritz. She retired after her Olympic victory and was awarded a C.B.E. in the Coronation Honours List.

AMOO, Eddie

Liverpool singer who was member of the Chants, underrated vocal harmony group of the 1960's who deserved a hit with their version of the standard 'I could write a book'. Formed Real Thing with brother Chris and had chart success in the 1970's. The brothers Amoo wrote the three song medley that completes the album '4 from 8', Liverpool 8, Children of the Ghetto and Stanhope Street, a melodic and unsentimental Mersey musical cameo.

ANGELIS, Michael

Michael Angelis as Mike Moriarty in Alan Bleasdale's "No Surrender"

Liverpool born actor and Boy from the Blackstuff (he played Chrissie in Bleasdale's blockbuster). In his early TV days was a "Liver Bird" boyfriend, and recently played Max in Carla Lane's "I Woke Up One Morning" on BBC TV.

ANGERS, Avril

18.4.22. Liverpool's funny lady was the first comedienne to have her own British TV series in the 1950's — "Dear Dotty". Has appeared in countless TV, film and stage parts since making her debut as a Tiller girl at 14 years of age. She is the daughter of Liverpool comedian, Harry Angers.

ANSDELL, Richard

1815-1885. Landseer's great rival, the Liverpool-born painter's "Hunted Slaves" is in the Walker Art Gallery.

ARGYLE THEATRE

Birkenhead's famous theatre, one of the leading Music Hall's in the country. All the great names played the Venue — Lauder, Formby, Chaplin and Stan Laurel — and it was the theatre chosen for the first broadcast of a live Music Hall performance. The first provincial venue to show moving pictures, it was bombed in 1940.

ARNOLD, Matthew

Poet, critic and educationalist, died in Liverpool in 1888, running to catch a tram. Was the service that bad?

ARTHUR, Patricia

BBC Brain of Sport winner in 1975, its inaugural year, still the only lady to have won the competition.

ASHES

Not the cricketing trophy, but the final gesture of love from supporters of Liverpool F.C. The practice over the years of scattering the cremated remains of the faithful, usually in the goalmouth at the Kop End, may explain The Reds spirited performance when attacking the Kop goal.

ASHLEY, April

The most famous and most publicised transexual was born George Jamieson on 29 April, 1935, at Smithdown Road

April Ashley

Hospital, Liverpool. George's Liverpudlian parents, father a Catholic, mother a Protestant, lived in Pitt Street, but when George was very young they moved to Teynham Crescent, Norris Green, Liverpool, to a new council house. George attended St. Teresa's School, Norris Green until he was 15, and early jobs were as a grocery delivery boy with Lundy's and as a deck hand with Furness Withy. After surviving the

tough environment of 1950's Liverpool, and a suicide attempt George moved to London and became "Toni April" working as a bacon slicer at Waitrose and a table wiper at Lyon's Corner House. After working as a dancer in Paris, a sex change operation in Casablanca followed and a name change by deed poll to April (after the month of her birth) Ashley (after Ashley Wilkes in "Gone with the Wind"). The glamorous April became a part of the swinging sixties scene, meeting Royalty, V.I.P.'s and stars of the entertainment world, John Lennon called her "Duchess". She modelled, had a brief role in the Crosby/Hope film "Road to Hong Kong" and married the Hon. Arthur Corbett. Corbett was the son of Lord Rowallen, the Chief Scout and Governor of Tasmania. His mother was a sister of Jo Grimond and the family fortune originated from the Brown and Polson cornflour company. She survived the Sunday People exposé "The Extraordinary Case of Top Model April Ashley" and a divorce from Corbett. In the 1970's, after overcoming drug reliance and a drink driving conviction (riding her bike in Chelsea) she left London for Hay-on-Wye. Her former ownership of a London restaurant inspired her to attend a catering course in Shrewsbury and a business studies course in Brecon. Her remarkable story, from Pitt Street to Sixties socialite and beyond is told in "April Ashley Odyssey" published in 1982, which she helped write with Duncan Fallowell.

ASHTONS

Family at War cast

The Liverpool family featured in the Granada TV drama shown in the 1970's, "A Family at War", set on Merseyside and created by John Finch. Edwin and Jean and children David, Margaret, Phillip, Robert and Freda.

ASHURST, Len
After representing his home City's boys' team, he went on to captain England Youth and to enjoy a long and loyal career as Sunderland's left back, eventually returning as Manager and taking them to the 1985 Milk Cup Final.
Sunderland lost, were relegated, and he joined Soccer's managerial casualties.

ASKEY, Arthur
One of Britain's best loved comedians, Arthur Bowden Askey was born 6 June 1900 at 29 Moses Street, Liverpool 8, in the area of Liverpool nicknamed "The Holy Land". Famous for the many catchphrases he used throughout his long career, he gave himself the title of "Big-hearted Arthur" and amongst many others were "Hello, Playmates", "Aye thank yew", and "Before your very eyes". He starred in the pre-war radio comedy landmark, "Band Waggon", and in many films and

on television. He was a much-loved pantomime Dame and his infectious and irrepressible humour never faded despite personal tragedies. Educated at Liverpool Institute, he worked as a clerk in the Liverpool Education Department before entering show business.
In the preface of his autiobiography he reflects upon a nostalgic visit back to Liverpool. "They've put a plaque on the wall of the house where I was born" he writes, "It says, condemned". His classic "Bee Song" sketch has been left on film for future generations. He died in 1982.

Arthur through the looking glass.

ATHENAEUM
Liverpool's is twenty seven years older than its London equivalent, and is now situated in Church Alley, after its move in 1928. Founded in 1797 by, amongst others, William Roscoe, it has one of the country's biggest and best private libraries.

ATKINSON, Ron
After managing Kettering Town, Cambridge United and West Bromich Albion, the Liverpool-born former player secured one of football's best jobs in 1981 when he became manager of Manchester United. It is not known whether his tailor or his jeweller moved with him.
He followed previous Liverpudlian influences as Tommy Cavanagh was for many years right-hand man at Old Trafford and, of course, the great Matt Busby was a former Liverpool FC wing half back.

B

BACK ENTRY DIDDLERS

Classic "Liverpool Echo" comic strip created by George Green, the Diddlers fired the imagination and fantasies of Liverpool's street footballers of the late 1940's and 1950's. Who could forget their star line-up: the bespectacled Jerry in goal, 'Erb, Nudger, Basher and their faithful follower, Maggie Ann?

BACKHOUSE, David

Award-winning Liverpool architect responsible for the Royal Insurance Company's development of Cavern Walks in Mathew Street. This most attractive development has quickly become a tourist 'must' with its range of specialist shops, pub, restaurants, club, as well as several floors of offices. The centrepiece is a life-size bronze statue of The Beatles by John Doubleday and a recent addition has been a statue of the great famine relief crusader, Bob Geldof.

Cavern Walks

BAKER, Ben Howard

Everton and England International goal-keeper, (3 full caps and 10 amateur), and all-round sportsman. He held the British High Jump record and was sixth in the Olympic High Jump final in Antwerp in 1920. He also played for Liverpool and Chelsea.

BAKER, Tom

Who is Tom Baker (?). Born in Scotland Road, he became TV's fourth Dr. Who in 1974, appearing in forty-two

BAINBRIDGE, Beryl

Award-winning Liverpool-born author of novels that include "A Quiet Life", "Injury Time", and "Young Adolf".
Winner of the Whitbread prize in 1977 (A Quiet Life) and the "Guardian" fiction award, and runner-up twice for the Booker prize for "The Dressmaker" and "The Bottle Factory Outing". Educated at Merchant Taylors, she was a juvenile character actress with the Liverpool Repertory Company. As an exile she once remarked that if the place was ever condemned to extinction "we'd all get the next train back".
A highly-individualistic lady, she has a full-sized dummy in her home called Neville Chamberlain. Her eight gramophone records for the famous radio programme, Desert Island Discs, were:

For Old Times' Sake — Layton and Johnston;
A Simple Little Melody — Richard Tauber;
My Foolish Heart — Margaret Whiting;
There's Something in Your Eyes, Madam —
    Geraldo and his Gaucho Tango Orchestra;
Ring, Telephone, Ring — Inkspots;
When You Where Sweet Sixteen — Fureys;
Sugar in my Bowl — George Melly;
Didn't We — Richard Harris.

episodes, and was top of the Madame Tussaud's popularity poll in 1980.
After seven years as a novice monk, was his part as the mad monk Rasputin in the film epic "Nicholas and Alexandra" type-casting?

Beryl Bainbridge

BALL, Alan

Everton and England midfield dynamo who was a World Cup hero in 1966. He made his Football League debut for Blackpool against Liverpool at Anfield in August, 1962, (Blackpool won 2-1) and joined Everton soon after his World Cup success, playing a significant role in the 1970 Championship win. A diminutive red-haired Lancastrian, the son of a footballing father, he played 62 times for England and also played for Arsenal and Southampton before becoming Portsmouth's manager. At one time, discussing his football experiences, he said there was nothing quite able to match "turning it on at Goodison in front of an appreciative audience".

BALL, John

1861-1940. Local golfer, a member of the Royal Liverpool Club, who was the first Englishman to win the British 'Open' in 1894 at Prestwick, and the first Amateur to win. Finished sixth in the 'Open' when only 15. When he was the professional at the Leasowe Club, he once did a round in dense fog, the wager being that he would score less than 90, not lose a ball and take less than three hours. He won his bet! He still holds the record for the most Amateur Championships (8).

BALMER, Jack

The first footballer to score three consecutive League hat-tricks. Playing for Liverpool, he scored 3 against Portsmouth at Anfield on 9th November, 1946, followed by 4 against

"Tash" Balmer. How long would the shorts be if he hadn't folded them over?

Derby County at the Baseball ground a week later. The following Saturday he scored another 3 against Arsenal, at Anfield.

A typical Bechers scene. Team Spirit falls and jockey D. Nicholson is about to arrive before his horse.

BARBER, Paul
Born in Liverpool in 1951, he played the letter-writing Wes in ITV's "The Brothers McGregor". Toured in the musical "Hair" in 1969/70 as one of the 'tribe' together with two other tribe members who found fame, Joan Armatrading and Floella Benjamin.

BASNETT, David
Former Trade Union Leader, General Secretary of the General, Municipal, Boilermakers and Allied Trades Union — Britain's third-largest union. Born 9th February, 1924, and educated at Quarry Bank High School, he has been a member of many significant committees, including Royal Commissions on Press and Penal Reforms. A member of the National Enterprise Board since 1973.

BEATLES, The
It could be argued that the zenith of 20th century British social history was attained on a sunny, suburban, psychedelic summer afternoon in Penny Lane, Liverpool, in the mid-1960's. The girls strode about confidently in colourful dresses several inches above their knees. The boys in winkle-pickers, money in their back pockets. Capital punishment had been abolished, laws had been passed that made life more bearable for homosexuals, jobs were available for those who wanted them. England were winning the World Cup and the Eurovision Song Contest and Harold Wilson was puffing away on his pipe. Mr. and Mrs. Sixties Citizen were on their way in their Mini to book their holiday in Majorca. And the Beatles were No.1 in the Hit Parade.
The scenario could be amended slightly, the place name changed. But the Beatles would always have to be Number 1 in the Hit Parade. Irrespective of their musical contribution, such was the social significance of the 'four lads who shook the world'. They achieved more concentrated fame than anyone before or since. And their music will always be evocative of the imagery of that sunny suburban Sixties afternoon.

BEAVAN, Margaret
Liverpool born teacher and reformer, daughter of a shipowner, she was responsible, in 1912, for Britain's first "open-air" hospital and convalescent home for children, both situated on the Wirral. A former Lord Mayor, she was Britain's second woman mayor, when elected in 1927.

BECHERS BROOK
World famous fence at the Aintree steeplechase course. It was named after Captain Becher who came to grief there in an early Grand National.

BEECHAM, Sir Thomas
1879-1961. Merseyside member of the 'pills and powder' family — who became one of the great conductors.
Founded the London Philharmonic Orchestra in 1932 and the Royal Philharmonic Orchestra in 1946. Was once reputed to have said to a lady cellist "Madam, you have between your legs an instrument capable of giving pleasure to thousands and all you can do is scratch it".

BELL, Tom
Tough and talented Liverpool TV and film actor, who has appeared in many film and TV roles, "Kings Royal", "Out", etc. Received rave reviews for "L-shaped Room" in the early days of his career. He also had the principal role in the Ted Whitehead TV Series, "Sweet Nothings", which was set in Liverpool.

BELLE VALE
The name given to the country's biggest pre-fab estate built by Liverpool Corporation shortly after the Second World War to ease the housing shortage. The 1159 "detached bungalows" were located on both sides of Childwall Valley Road and schools, shops, churches and community centres were built on the estate. They survived for over 20 years.

BELLINGHAM, John
Bankrupt Liverpudlian who vented his grievance against society with the only assassination of a British Prime Minister Spencer Perceval, in the lobby of the House of Commons in 1812.
He was, in fact, apprehended by Liverpool M.P., Bamber Gascoigne, ancestor of TV's "University Challenge" host. The Merseyside connection was completed when Robert Banks Jenkinson, Second Earl of Liverpool, succeeded Perceval as Premier for the subsequent fifteen years.

BENNETT, Billy
Famous Liverpool Music Hall comic of pre-war days. "I represent the common people", said Bennett, "and there is no one more common than me".
His stage act usually consisted of a dead-pan delivery of monologues, finishing with, "That's the end of that one", before starting another. He dressed on stage in an ill-fitting dinner suit with a red sash and . . . carpet slippers.

BERT
Fictious Beatle of the Willy Russell play, "John Paul George Ringo . . . and Bert". The play, which was performed at the Everyman in 1974, was transferred to the Lyric in London and gave early opportunities to Bernard Hill (John), Trevor Eve (Paul), Anthony Sher (Ringo) and Barbara Dickson, the Scots lass with a Scouse mam.

BEST, Johnny Snr. & Son
Merseyside's best-known boxing promoters, responsible for many Stadium attractions up to the 1960's.

Johnny Best Senior (standing) with, from left to right, Jimmy Walsh of Chester, and Liverpool's Nel Tarleton and Ernie Roderick.

Pete Best with George, Paul and John at the Cavern.

BEST, Pete

The drummer that missed the beat. Was controversially dropped by Brian Epstein in favour of one Richard Starkey (Ringo Starr) on the threshold of Beatlemania.

BIFFIN, Sarah

1784-1850. Celebrated armless Liverpool painter reputed to be just 3 feet tall, and naturally well-known for her miniatures. Among her patrons were the Royal Family. She died at 8 Duke Street.

The Big House

BIG HOUSE, The

(The Vines) Lime Street. One of the big four of Liverpool's magnificent Edwardian pub masterpieces. The others are The Phil, The Central and The Crown. A truly majestic and opulent drinking emporium.

BIG THREE

Influential Mersey beat group of the 1960's who didn't quite make it nationally, though they had hits with "Some Other Guy", "By the Way", and the EP, "Live at the Cavern".

BINGHAM, Billy

Former Everton winger and manager who, having led N. Ireland to the 1982 World Cup Finals, achieved the tremendous feat of leading them to the 1986 Mexico World Cup Finals. No doubt Billy's success as manager is helped considerably by the fact that he still lives on Merseyside, and is able to spy on the two local giants when seeking inspiration.

BIRKENHEAD, Earl of

1872-1930. F. E. Smith, locally-born and educated. He rose rapidly to the Bar and after entering Parliament as a Conservative in 1906, earned a reputation as a brilliant and witty orator. Nicknamed "The Galloper", he was responsible for the Law of Property Act, 1922 a significant change in the law of property which rid the system of many archaisms. His maiden parliamentary speech on 12th May, 1906 — perhaps the most famous maiden speech in parliamentary history — moved his fellow townie, J. L. Girvin, to comment, "He spoke for an hour and put the House in his pocket".

Surprise, Surprise — how's this for a 'Blind Date' at the Cavern.

BIRKENHEAD PARK R.U.F.C.

At times during their long history, founded 1871, they have been one of the strongest teams in the country. Perhaps the best known of the many international players they have produced was H. M. Locke, who played 12 times for England during vintage years of the 1920's. His name wasn't a clue to his position; he was a centre. He also played in the Rugby School 'Centenary Match' in 1923 when a combined England/Wales XV beat Scotland/Ireland 21-16.

BIRRELL, Rt. Hon. Augustine

Born at Wavertree, Liverpool, in 1850, he was First Secretary to Ireland between 1907-1916. He was also an author and essayist of some note, and provided critical works on Hazlitt and Marvell as well as a volume of essays, 'Obiter Dicta'. He died in 1933.

BLACK, Capt. T. Campbell

Flyer and hero of the London-Melbourne Air Race in 1934. Together with C.W.A. Scott he won the race in a D.H. Comet in the record time of 2 days 22 hours 54 minutes and 18 seconds. Capt. Campbell Black was tragically killed at Speke Aerodrome in September, 1936, when his plane, "Miss Liverpool I", was in collision with an RAF plane whilst taxiing. "Miss Liverpool" had been presented by John Moores and was to be used in the London-Johannesburg race later that year. The race was eventually won by C. W. A. Scott with a different plane, a Percival Vega Gull.

BLACK, Cilla

Liverpool's most popular songstress was a cloakroom girl at the Cavern Club in the early 1960's and eventually joined Brian Epstein's 'stable' of recording stars. Born Priscilla Maria Veronica White, in the Scotland Road area of Liverpool, she had a string of big hits including "Anyone who had a Heart", "You're my World" and "Step Inside Love" but perhaps her most memorable recording is her moving version of "Liverpool Lullaby" ('Oh, you are a mucky kid').
Several successful TV series endeared her to the British public as a family entertainer, and her natural charm and humour have made her a favourite for over twenty years.
She is currently top of the love parade stealing hearts and laughs on T.V.'s 'Blind Date' and 'Surprise, Surprise'.

BLEASDALE, Alan

Award winning playwright who draws upon his home city for much of his inspiration. His descriptions of Liverpool have included "the city is like a film set" and "the ballroom of the Titanic". Will always be remembered for his brilliant TV plays, "The Boys from the Blackstuff", which enthralled the nation on five successive Sundays in Autumn 1982, and achieved the distinction of being the quickest-ever repeated series, when it was broadcast again in the early weeks of 1983. The series was a brilliant tour-de-force combining the humour, character and tragedy of modern-day Liverpool and a powerful social comment on the despair of unemployment and deprivation in the inner city.
Perhaps the highest accolade he received on its social impact was the parallel of a 'modern-day Dickens'.
Other successful stage and TV plays include the award-winning "Are You Lonesome Tonight?".
The former Huyton teacher and Liverpool F.C. follower received further acclaim with his full-length cinema film

Alan Bleasdale

Andrew Schofield as Scully in the televised version of the programme that Bleasdale created for local radio. The Evertonian is Trevor Steven.

debut, "No Surrender", based on sectarian senior citizens in his home city. His TV screen adaptation of the 'Monocled Mutineer' in Autumn, 1986, caused controversy but much critical and popular acclaim.

Monday morning, August 28th 1939
Please be sure to send your child
with a packed bag and the
GAS MASK (in box) at 9 o'clock.
Children must come
to school this morning
and this afternoon as
usual.
Scholars will not be take
to the station today.
Put what you can in the
bags and don't worry.

The Leaving of Liverpool. Merseyside children being evacuated 28 August, 1939.

Those who stayed behind wore their gas masks.

BLITZ

Measured by the weight and numbers of attacks, Merseyside was Hitler's number one target outside London during the Second World War. Between August 1940 and January 1942, 3,966 Merseysiders were killed and over 3,000 seriously-injured in air raids on the City, almost 70 in total. In Liverpool alone, over 120,000 houses were damaged. The worst raids took place in early May 1941, the infamous 'May Blitz' when 1,453 people were killed in Liverpool and over 1,000 seriously injured. Liverpool, as the war's most strategic port, faced the Luftwaffe for eight consecutive nights during that May onslaught. Within three days of the end of that battering, every shift at the docks was working normally.

St. Luke's Church stands today as a stark and poignant reminder of those days and as a testimony to those Merseysiders who lived through those grim times.

Liverpool street scene, 1940. The bomb crater measured 18 feet wide and 12 feet deep.

The tenant of this Liverpool house was shaving when a bomb struck his home. He walked outside and, minutes later, the house collapsed.

Some moved out in a hurry . . . With their slippers and a picture of the Royal Family.

A view from Paradise Street towards the Queen Victoria Monument in 1941.

Queen Victoria Monument, 1946.

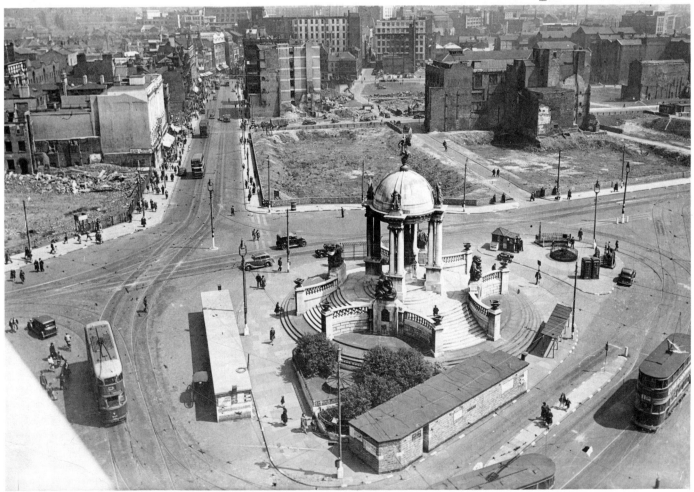

The junction of Church Street and Parker Street, 1940.

BLOW THE MAN DOWN

Perhaps Liverpool's oldest famous song, the sea shanty was composed in the 17th Century at the time of Liverpool's privateers. Unaware of the composers — maybe Bosun Lennon and his Mate McCartney.

BLUECOAT CHAMBERS

Beautiful city-centre building built in 1717 and originally intended for use as a hospital, it was used for the education of poor children. The building was saved from the threat of demolition in 1927 by a donation of £18,000 from Mr. W. E. Corlett, a Liverpool solicitor, made anonymously at the time. The building was restored after war damage and is now used as an arts centre.

BOARDMAN, Stan

Rising comedy star with increasing amount of TV exposure. Unlike Basil Fawlty, Stan mentions the 'Germans' frequently and always gets away with it. He was on Liverpool FC's books as an amateur.

BOHT, Jean

Liverpool actress, Playhouse trained, who has featured in Carla Lane's "I Woke Up One Morning" and "Bread". She played Rosa's mum in the first named and the matriachal Nellie Boswell in "Bread". She is married to American composer and conductor Carl Davis.

BOOTH, Anthony

The Scouse 'git' of Johnny Speight's 'Till Death Us Do Part' BBC TV series in which he had to contend with Alf Garnet's bigotry and support of West Ham United. As Liverpool usually beat West Ham, it was the bigotry that gave him the most problems. He married Pat Phoenix, Coronation Street's Elsie Tanner in 1986's most poignant wedding ceremony, in hospital at Cheadle a week before she died.

BOOTH, Charles

1840-1916. The Liverpool shipowner who wrote the mammoth social documents, "Life and Labour of People in London", which roused many consciences when published between 1891-1903 and played a major contribution to the passing of the Old Age Pensions Act of 1908.

BOSWELLS The

Lovable rogue Liverpool family of Carla Lane's BBC TV series "Bread" joining forces in the family business of survival. Apart from Nellie (Jean Boht) there's Adrian, Joey, Aveline, Billy and Jack (Victor McGuire who played Ray in "What Now?").

BOTHAM, Ian

England's cricket superstar and former Scunthorpe United reserve centre forward was born at Heswall, 24th November, 1955. His cricketing exploits are legend, took John O'Groats and Lands End in his stride, and any number of Shredded Wheat pose him no problems.

BOULT, Sir Adrian

1889-1983. Son of Liverpool shipbroker, he became one of the country's leading conductors. He was the first Director of the BBC Symphony Orchestra in 1930 and became their principal conductor.

Adrian Boult

BOWE, Colette

High-ranking Civil Servant born in Speke, Liverpool, in 1946 and educated at Druids Cross School, Notre Dame High School and Oxford University. The Director of Information at the Dept. of Trade and Industry, she was named in the Commons by Tam Dalyell as the civil servant who leaked certain information during the "Westland Affair" damaging to Michael Heseltine, which ultimately led to the resignations of Heseltine and Leon Brittan.

BRABEN, Eddie

Liverpool born scriptwriter who has written for Radio and TV but probably best known for his contributions to the "Morecambe and Wise Show" when that show attracted massive viewing audiences in the 1970's.

His radio creation 'The Show with Eight Legs' really put him on his feet and the World Premiere of his stage show "The Divvies are Coming" was at the Playhouse at Christmas 1985.

BRADDOCK, Mrs. Elizabeth Margaret — "Bessie"

Much-loved Liverpool Labour MP, a big lady in more ways than one, she represented her constituency, Liverpool

19

Exchange, from 1945-1969 and was a great champion of the underprivileged and downtrodden. Born September 24th, 1899, she attended her first political meeting when just 3 weeks old. Elected to Liverpool City Council in 1930, she was a full-time member of the City's ambulance service during the war. She campaigned in Parliament for better housing, hospitals, maternity and child welfare. She had a personal reason for her campaign for outsize clothes for women — she measured 50-40-50 for much of her parliamentary career despite being just 5'2".

Quintin Hogg described her as his favourite pin-up, but she was the target of many unkind jibes, the most famous of which was Churchill's caustic reply to her accusation, "You are drunk, Mr. Churchill," to which he replied, "Yes, Mrs. Braddock, but you are ugly and I shall be sober in the morning".

She was the first woman MP to be suspended from the House, for refusing to resume her seat during a debate, and her love of boxing inspired her to invite World Champion Floyd Paterson to the Commons for lunch.

Her husband, John, was also very attractive in local politics and for several decades their name was synonymous with Liverpool political life. She lived in Zig-Zag Road, West Derby, and was made a Freeman of the City in the year she died, 1970.

BRASSEY, Thomas
1805-1870. Locally born builder and railway contractor responsible for building all of France's major railways.

BRODIE, JOHN ALEXANDER
1858-1934. John Brodie invented the goal nets introduced to Association Football in 1892. Liverpool City Engineer, he has an avenue named after him in Mossley Hill.
He was also involved in the construction of the first Mersey Tunnel and the development of Queens Drive.

BROOKSIDE
Channel 4's most popular programme and something of a cult, created by Liverpudlian Phil Redmond and a vehicle for many fine Liverpool character actors.
The action takes place on part of a 'real' housing estate at Croxteth Park and the first episode was shown on Channel 4's first night in November 1982.

BROWN, Faith
Liverpool-born comedy impressionist who appears regularly on TV and has been featured in her own TV series. Cannot recall seeing her do a Dolly Parton impression, but she has all the natural equipment for it . . .
Under her real name Irene Carroll, was a member of family singing group 'The Carrolls' in the 1960's.

BRUNNER, John
Born in Everton in 1842, he founded a chemical works in Northwich which was the forerunner of I.C.I.

BRUSSELS
The venue for the most tragic event in Merseyside's sporting history, when, after crowd disturbances prior to the Liverpool-Juventus European Cup Final, on 29th May, 1985, at the Heysel Stadium, thirty-nine people mostly Italians died and many others were injured. The incident and tragic aftermath culminated years of English soccer crowd problems and consequently a world-wide ban was enforced.

BRYAN, Dora
North country character actress who had a hit record with "All I Want for Christmas is a Beatle" in 1963. At the time she reflected the world's Christmas wish.

BUTLER, Billy
Merseyside's most popular local radio personality who has defiantly supported Everton FC even when they were on different wavelengths. His 'phone-in show on BBC Radio Merseyside has produced many natural comic classics "Go on Billy, give us a clue".
A former Cavern DJ and TV trivia expert he continually advises his listeners to "Hold Their Plums".

BUTLER, Josephine
1828-1906. A great worker to improve conditions for women in 19th century Liverpool, particularly the plight of thousands of prostitutes. She founded Homes for the poor and sick and was founder of the International Society of State Regulated Vice, which held its first Congress in Liverpool in 1875. She was the wife of the principal of the Liverpool College for Boys.

BURGESS, Brian
Liverpool born sculptor whose most notable local work is "Christ Upon an Ass" situated in St. Nicholas's churchyard facing the Atlantic Tower Hotel. A stunning work, most worthy to adorn Liverpool's Parish church, depicts Christ wearing beads and a 'Ban the Bomb' medallion.

Faith Brown

C

CABBAGE HALL
Former cinema opened in 1914 with surely the most unusual name in Britain. It is now used for the headquarters of Liverpool F.C. Supporters' Club but the name is retained by the pub opposite.

CALDER STONES
Originally sited outside the Menlove Avenue gates of the park, six stones believed to be remains of a prehistoric ring and erected and carved by a Turanian race.

CAMEO CINEMA
Webster Road, Liverpool 7. The scene of the notorious Cameo murder in 1949, now a lighting warehouse.
George Kelly was hanged at Walton Gaol for the the murder of Leonard Thomas, the cinema's manager.

CAMMELL LAIRD
World-renowned shipbuilding yard founded by William Laird, a Scotsman, who arrived South in 1810. He started the shipyard, and was largely responsible for the growth of modern Birkenhead. The yard's list of achievements is formidable — the first iron gunboat and warship in the world (The Guadeloupe), the first screw steamer (Robert F. Stockton), the largest wet dock in Britain (1900), the first British submarine (1915), the longest dredger in the world (1908 — The Leviathan), the first-ever British welded ship (1920). Among the famous names were HMS Chester, HMS Devonshire (the Navy's first guided missile ship), RMS Mauretania and HMS Ark Royal, the largest ship to be launched on the Mersey.
And to the well-known Mersey quiz question, "Who painted the Mona Lisa?" "Cammell Lairds, they paint all the Isle of Man boats!"

CAMPBELL, Bobby
Born in Scotland Road he lived in Penrhyn Street, Liverpool. Played for his home town club Liverpool, in the 1950's and went on to manage Fulham and Portsmouth.

Part of the crowd that gathered outside St. George's Hall to wait for the Cameo murder verdict on 28 January, 1950.

The launching of the Ark Royal, 3 May, 1950.

CAREY, John

Popular Everton manager of the 1950's and early 1960's who had a distinguished playing career with Manchester United and Republic of Ireland. His eventual dismissal from Everton in April 1961, was for a long time the cause of speculation and debate. Did it really take place in a taxi?

CARTER, Philip David

Everton F.C. chairman since 1978, appointed Chairman Merseyside Tourism Board and President of the Football League in 1986. Educated at Waterloo Grammar School, he has been Managing Director, Littlewoods Organisation, and President, European Mail Order Trade Association. Awarded CBE.

As Chairman of Everton and a former Managing Director of Littlewoods, will no doubt be hoping his team can be the first winners of the Littlewood Cup (replacing the Milk Cup) in 1987.

CATHEDRALS

The city with a cathedral to spare, and either one a magnificent and contrasting architectural gem. The Anglican cathedral, with a tower 466 ft above sea level, is the largest Anglican church in the world, twice as big as St. Pauls, and the fifth largest of any denomination in the world. The foundation stone was laid by Edward VII in 1904, consecrated in 1924 with George V in attendance and completed in October 1978 in the presence of Elizabeth II. The architect was Sir Giles Gilbert Scott — a Catholic — just 21 years old when his design was accepted.

The Metropolitan Cathedral of Christ the King was consecrated on Whit Sunday, 14th May, 1967, 114 years after a Catholic cathedral in the city was first conceived.

After many frustrating starts and non-completions, Cardinal Heenan, when Archbishop of Liverpool, realised that more modern methods were required in order that the building be completed. Sir Frederick Gibberd, a non-Catholic, was responsible for the winning design to be built within the reduced budget available. The Lutyens crypt, part of the original grandiose scheme, has been incorporated in the completion of one of the most distinctive buildings in modern-day Britain.

The two cathedrals, linked by a street called Hope, have in their present custodians, Archbishop Worlock and Bishop Sheppard, two men who have worked closely together to reconcile the differences of religious prejudice that have existed in Liverpool. Both give a prominent ecclesiastical lead in helping to combat Liverpool's difficulties of today.

CATTERICK, Harry

Everton FC manager and former centre forward who guided the club to championship success in 1963 and 1970, and to an FA Cup Final win in 1966. He joined the club from Sheffield Wednesday and despite his successes was not always popular with the Everton faithful, particularly when dropping the revered Alex Young from the side. He was once attacked by his own supporters on an ill-fated afternoon after a match against Blackpool at Bloomfield Road. Nicknamed 'Black Harry' he was a sober, executive-style manager in sharp contrast to his principal adversary of Sixties Mersey football, the ebullient Shankly. He died, tragically early, at the end of an F.A. Cup tie between Everton and Ipswich in March, 1985.

22

CAVANAGH, Eddie

In 1966 during the Everton and Sheffield Wednesday Cup Final, when the trademark of football fans was enthusiasm, and the media had a sense of humour, Eddie, in a state of delirium, ran on to the pitch to celebrate an Everton goal. He left policeman sprawling with his coat tails and was carried off in a state of euphoria to the amusement of all. Even the police were smiling!

An Everton fanatic and a club steward, his son was named after his godfather . . . Alan Ball Cavanagh.

CAVERN, The

The most famous beat club in the world has now, sadly, closed its doors, though the memories and melodies linger on. 10 Mathew Street opened as a jazz club on 16th January, 1957, its ex-warehouse, cave-like atmosphere evoking comparisons with the Parisien left bank jazz clubs. By 1960, when Ray McFall had taken up ownership, modern and traditional jazz sessions were being shared with beat and country-and-western performances. And then, on Tuesday 21st March, 1961, a group made its debut — the first of 292 appearances at the Cavern — which made the cellar's fame everlasting . . . the Beatles.

All the famous Mersey groups of the day appeared there, as well as many of the world's leading rock names. Little Richard, Gene Vincent, Rolling Stones, Sonny Boy Williamson and many many more. The clubs long time resident Dee Jay and compere Bob Wooler, a great supporter and influence on the Mersey groups of that era, went on to introduce a weekly Radio Luxembourg programme, "Sunday Night at the Cavern".

A reconstruction of the old club was incorporated on the same site as part of the Cavern Walks development.

The Cavern with Bob Wooler.

CAZNEAU STREET

Did you hear the one about the policeman who found a dead horse in Cazaneau Street? He dragged it half-a-mile to Scotland Road because he couldn't spell Cazneaux Street.

CHADS, The

Liverpool's speedway team that raced at Stanley Stadium, Prescot Road, between 1928-1960. Among their best-known riders were Ginger Lees, Oliver Hart, and their highest-points scorer, Harry Welch. They did, however, give a free transfer to Peter Craven who signed for Belle Vue.

CHAPPELL, Annette

Dancer and ballerina born in Liverpool, 1929. She was with the Ballet Rambert between 1944-49, eventually becoming a principal ballerina. She has taught in England and on the continent, principally in Munich.

CHEGWIN, Keith

Born 17.1.57. "Cheggers" is a popular children's TV and radio entertainer. Born in Liverpool, he married Maggie Philbin in 1981 whom he'd met whilst working on the same TV show.

He is the brother of Radio One and Top of the Pops D.J., Janice Long, and was previously a member of pop group, 'Kenny'.

Action at Stanley Stadium in 1951. Craven receives the World Championship trophy from Norman Wisdom in 1962. Runner-up Barry Briggs is on the right and 3rd-placed Ove Fundin on the left.

CHRISTIAN, Lizzie

Well-known Liverpool flower-seller, who was a familiar feature of City life for many years, at her stall near the former St. Johns Market, in Clayton Square.

Janice Long

CHRISTIANSEN, Arthur

1904-1963. Merseyside headliner and one of the most famous Fleet Street editors, he edited the Daily Express between 1933-1958, some of the newspaper's most progressive years. Educated at Wallasey Grammar School, he was a reporter on the Wallasey and Wirral Chronicle and was London editor for the old Liverpool Evening Express.

Hugh Cudlipp described him as "the patron Saint of Urgency". His autobiography "Headlines all my life" was published in 1961.

CITRINE, Walter M.

Lord Citrine. Born in Wallasey, he was General Secretary of the T.U.C. (1926-46) and President of the World Federation of Trade Unions (1945-46). He was knighted in 1935 and made a peer in 1946.

CLARKE, Frank

A contender for 'Liverpudlian of 1985' after his tremendous achievement in the creating of one of the best films of the year 'Letter to Brezhnev' ably supported by a cast of friends and family.

Peter Firth and Alexandra Pigg in a scene from the film "Letter to Brezhnev".

Sister Margi, along with Alexandra Pigg, were joint winners of 'The Standard' film award for best newcomers.

CLOUGH, Arthur Hugh

1819-1861. Arthur Hugh, born at 74 Rodney Street (though the plaque is outside No.9) the son of a Liverpool cotton merchant. He was educated at Rugby at the time of Dr. Arnold, and his poetry includes: "Amours de Voyage", "Dipsychus", "The Latest Decalogue", "Peschiera" — *Better to have fought and lost than never to have fought at all* — "Say not the Struggle naught availeth" and "Where lies the Land" — *But westward, look, the land is bright.*

His sister Anne was a great champion of womens' rights, particularly in higher education. She founded and was first principal at Newnham College, Cambridge.

CODMAN, 'Professor'

A family who for several generations have entertained thousands of Liverpool children with brutality, sadism, sexism and all the other ingredients of a Punch-and-Judy show. Visitors to the city, seeking the location of the gigantic classical edifice of St. George's Hall, were frequently advised to look behind Codman's Punch and Judy stand.

COGGER

Liverpool slang for Roman Catholic, left footer.

COHEN, Avi

Israeli international signed by Liverpool FC who, to Paisley's relief, was able to play on the Sabbath (Saturday).

COHEN, Henry

Lord Cohen of Birkenhead, 21.2.1900-7.8.1977. Brilliant physician and diagnostician, the first physician from the provinces to be made a peer (1956). Born in Birkenhead, from a poor Jewish home, he was educated at Birkenhead Institute and the Universities of Liverpool, London and Paris. He was consulting physician at Liverpool Royal Infirmary for 41 years from 1924. Among many distinguished positions he held was: President of the British Medical Association and President of the Royal Society of Health. He was principal adviser in the early days of the National Health Service. He remained devoted to Merseyside, and played an active role in the cultural and social progress of the area, living in Liverpool for most of his life. He was made a Freeman of Birkenhead in 1956 and Honorary Freeman of Liverpool in 1970.

COLLINS, Lewis
Birkenhead-born actor best known for his role as Bodie in TV's "The Professionals", he was formerly a member of the Mojos, a Mersey group of the 1960's. In his early TV days he played Gavin in Granada's "The Cuckoo Waltz".

CONNY ONNY
Scouse nickname for condensed milk.
For Liverpool/Everton fudge you need the following ingredients:
4 ozs butter
4 tablespoons water
2 tablespoons golden syrup
1¼lb caster sugar
small can of conny onny
teaspoon either red or blue food colouring
Put the butter, water, syrup and sugar in a large heavy based pan and heat gently until sugar has dissolved. Add the conny onny bring to the boil and then add a few drops of the appropriate food colouring and beat well until thick.
For best results serve after a home victory at either Goodison Park or Anfield.

CONTEH, John
Vintage Liverpudlian boxer with the full range of skills. He won the world light-heavyweight title in 1974 after a distinguished amateur career. His charismatic personality did not always endear him to the establishment, and as a restaurateur, he did not go the distance with Egon Ronay. Accomplished all rounder, had his superstar status confirmed with his success in TV's "Superstar" series which he won

COPE, Kenneth
Liverpool-born TV and film actor who for several years featured on TV's "That Was The Week That Was", and "Randall and Hopkirk (deceased)". He played Jed Stone in Coronation Street. Opened a restaurant, "Martha's Kitchen", in Watlington, Oxon, in 1974.

COPPELL, Steve
Liverpool-born England and Manchester United winger who started his career with Tranmere Rovers. Obtained a Degree in Economics at Liverpool University but his football could hardly be described as economical, as he was one of the hardest-working wingers of recent times. His playing career ended prematurely in 1983, but he went on to be Chairman of the PFA and Manager of Crystal Palace F.C.

COSTELLO, Elvis
Born Declan MacManus in 1955, the son of Ross, popular Merseyside balladeer of Light Programme days, who tied with Billy Fury for tenth place in the 1961 'Melody Maker' best singer poll.
Elvis emerged as the most distinctive writer/performer of the 'new wave' music of the late 1970's. His first chart entry was 'Watching the Detectives' in 1977 and 'Oliver's Army' reached No.2 in 1979. 'A Good Year for the Roses' was one of the best songs of 1981, and his appearances with the Attractions were sell-outs. He has produced albums for The Specials and Squeeze and had a major role in Alan Bleasdale's TV series of 'Scully'. His composition 'Girls Talk' was a top ten hit for Dave Edmunds in 1979, and Linda Ronstadt has recorded several of his songs.

John Conteh on his way to winning the World Title against Jorge Ahumada.

in 1974. Transferred from the ring to the stage and appeared in Willy Russell's musical play "Blood Brothers" which produced great critical and popular acclaim and the hit song "Say It Isn't So".

COTTERELL, Lol
Bakery delivery man who made the 'Big Time'. He achieved his ambition by playing for the team he supported and to whom he made his bread and pie deliveries. He played in

Tommy Smith's testimonial match on Friday 27th May, 1977, just two days after Liverpool's European Cup triumph in Rome. The sequence was filmed for Esther Rantzen's BBC TV show 'The Big Time' as 35,694 fans filled Anfield for the match against Bobby Charlton's XI (9-9). Poor Lol, the pie man turned out to be a puddin', he missed two penalties!!

CRANE, Walter
1845-1915. Liverpool-born portrait and landscape painter and the best book illustrator of his day. He was President of The Royal College of Art.

CRANSTON, Kenneth
Born in Aigburth, Liverpool in 1917 he captained the England cricket team in one Test against the West Indies in 1947/48. He only played two full first class seasons, captaining Lancashire in 1947 and 1948.

CRAVEN, Peter
Diminutive Liverpool born speedway rider, who won the World Title in 1955 and 1962. A fearless and exciting rider he was known as the 'Mighty Atom' and the only Englishman to win the title more than once. His career came to a tragic and premature end in 1963. Riding in Edinburgh, he crashed into a safety fence while attempting to avoid a fallen rider. He died shortly afterwards.

CRAWSHAW, Richard
Lord Crawshaw of Aintree. Former Labour MP for Toxteth and Liverpool City Councillor who was the SDP's first nominated life peer in 1985. He was Toxteth's MP for 19 years, deputy speaker and a barrister and a great marathon walker for charity. He died in July 1986.

CREEVEY, Thomas
Born in Liverpool the son of a slave trader, he was appointed Treasurer of the Ordnance in 1830. His letters and journals provide an interesting insight into 19th century society.

CREUS, Julian
British weightlifting champion and a record holder for the Bantam and Featherweight classes. He won an Olympic silver medal in 1948.

CRICHTON, Charles
Merseyside-born, Wallasey, 1910. Film director of such Ealing classics as 'Lavender Hill Mob', 'Titfield Thunderbolt', and later on TV, 'The Avengers' and 'DangerMan'.

CROOKE, Muriel
She started the country's first kennel and training school for guide dogs for the blind in 1931. Born in Wallasey, her innovation in New Brighton led to a national institution.

CROSSWORD PUZZLE
Liverpool born Arthur Wynne invented and compiled the first crossword which appeared in the New York World Weekend Supplement on 21st December, 1913.

CROW
Liverpudlian superstar of 'Saturday Superstore' on TV. This bird, like the City's Liver Birds, appears to be a non-flyer.

CUNARD, Samuel Sir
Arrived in Britain from Canada and along with George Burns and Liverpudlian David MacIver founded the British and North American Royal Mail Steam Packet Company, later to become the world-famous shipping line that bore his name. The first scheduled trans-atlantic service was started from Liverpool to Boston in 1840, the wooden paddle steamer, Britannia, taking two weeks for the crossing with 63 passengers aboard. During the First World War the company lost 22 ships through enemy action, including the Lusitania, the sinking of which precipitated the entry of the USA into the war. The liner was sunk without warning by a German submarine with a loss of over 1300 lives. The great Cunard liners Mauretania and the Queens, Mary and Elizabeth, were registered in Liverpool and carried the City's name on their sterns throughout their Blue Riband careers. The Cunard building, a magnificent Italianate palace, was built during the First World War and although no longer owned by Cunard, the building forms an integral part of Liverpool's famous waterfront. Cunard, a giant name at the head of the other names who started their great shipping lines in Liverpool, Holt, Booth, Bibby, Brocklebank, Harrison and Ismay . . .

CURRIE, Edwina
The Conservative MP for North Derbyshire is a shopkeeper's daughter from Liverpool. There's another shopkeeper's daughter in politics who went even further than North Derbyshire. Now who was that?

Shortly after her appointment as Junior Health Minister in September 1986, Mrs. Currie caused considerable controversy with her remarks about Northerners diets and they weren't 'Let them eat cake'.

CYCLING
As befits a city that had the first cycling club in the country — Liverpool Velocipedes (founded 1867) — the area has provided a string of well known cyclists, Joey McLaughlin being most notable.

The late Eddie Soens, as well as being a Liverpool cycle retailer, was for many years a national administrator.

Doug Dailey of the Kirkby Cycling Club, a former champion was appointed National Coach and was due to take on his new job in November 1986, Paul McHugh, 21-year old Liverpudlian is British amateur sprint champion and record holder.

SCOUSEOLOGY CROSSWORD

CLUES

ACROSS

1 & 2. He used his loaf, but Tommy and Esther benefitted (3, 8)

3. A Starr backing group (8)

4. Scouse Fernandel (7)

5 & 6. He didn't bomb our chippy but he got a Final break (5, 5)

7. Son of John, partner to Ivy (5)

8. Many a cross word between him and 'youse'
From this man who's opposed to lose (5)

9. A peach of a comedian, the ''toast of the town'' (5)

21. It's that man again (4)

22. Overtures of Marauding Devils (3)

26 & 27. The Flying Pig (5) (8)

DOWN

10. Sixties band 'not more than five' (8)

11. ＿ ＿ ＿ ＿ ＿ ＿ ＿ ＿ explodes (8)

12. 86 is his year, this Nigerian Liverpool-based boxer who is sadly no longer with us (5)

13. Hamburg's response to the Beatles (7)

14. Johnny's still searching for his backing group in a pub by the Kop (6). Now they've changed the name of the pub!! (6)

15 & 16. Soggy Helen (3, 5)

17. Sixties' Tommy was no slowcoach (7)

18, 19 & Colourful Anglo-Irish cocktail
20. (5, 3, 3)

23. Meet Ron G. on a ferry to a district on the Wirral (8)

24. ＿ ＿ ＿ ＿ ＿ Piazzas (5)

25. The place where Maggie cruised (7)

Correct solution to SCOUSEOLOGY CROSSWORD on Readers' Reply Page at the back of this book.

D

DALGLISH, Kenny

Britain's best footballer of recent years is a Glaswegian who signed for Liverpool FC in August 1977 to replace Kevin Keegan. He scored the winning goal in the 1978 European Cup Final against Bruges and was voted Footballer of the Year in 1979 and 1983. He has a record number of Scottish caps, becoming the first Scot to play 100 times for his country in 1986, and is the only player to score a hundred goals in both Scottish and English football. He combines high skill and vision with total commitment and clinical, frequently brilliant, finishing. Described as Liverpool's best-ever buy. Among the many admirers who attended TV's "This is Your Life" tribute was Petula Clark, her husband and son, who arrived from their home in Switzerland where they are devotees of King Kenny. His appointment as player/manager in 1985 was greeted with scepticism in some quarters but he led Liverpool to their historic double of League and F.A. Cup and was voted Bell's Manager of the Year. The only disappointment to a remarkable season was his withdrawal from the Scottish World Cup squad through injury, which prevented him from appearing in his fourth World Cup Finals. Strangely, he made his debut in a Liverpool shirt when he played for the "B" team against Southport on 20th August 1966 when on a two-week trial.

Ronnie Moran, Bob Paisley and Roy Evans toast Kenny in the Anfield Boot Room after the news that he was to be made a Freeman of Glasgow.

DANCER, Benjamin

Responsible for first microphotograph (1839) and the first photograph developing and printing service, which started in Liverpool in 1840.

DANIELS, Pauline

The only lady to have a spot on Granada TV's "The Comedians" was Liverpool's Pauline. The programme was a vehicle for the talents of many other Merseyside comics: George Roper, Mike Burton, Steve Faye. Pauline took part in the female comedy workshop for aspiring lady comics which was a part of the first "Festival of Comedy". This took place in July 1986, sponsored by D.E.R.

DAVID, Roy

Liverpudlian writer, former Daily Post journalist, who, after considerable research, published "The Shergar Mystery" — an exposé on the missing racehorse affair. Former Liverpool Playhouse director, Bill Morrison, wrote a TV documentary play on the horse's disappearance which was televised in March 1986.

Previous Liverpudlian theories regarding the Shergar disappearance included the popular notion that the horse was grazing in Liverpool FC's goalmouth at Anfield. This was a result of the club's dominance at Anfield in setting a British record of playing 85 consecutive home matches without defeat — 63 League games, 9 League Cup, 6 FA Cup, 6 European Cup and 1 Super Cup ensuring most of the action took place in their opponents' goalmouth.

DAVIES, Dickie

Sartorially elegant, former purser with Cunard, his Merseyside-born smile presented for many years ITV's "World of Sport".

DEAN, Bill

Well known Liverpudlian TV and film actor now receiving regular exposure as Harry Cross in "Brookside".

DEAN, William Ralph

The legendary 'Dixie' Dean is Merseyside's most famous all-time soccer son. Born in Birkenhead he played for Everton in their great days of the 1920's and 1930's. In 1927/28 he scored 60 goals in 39 First Division matches, a record likely to stand for ever. An accident left him with a tin plate in his skull and, although he was a tremendous header of a ball, most of his goals were scored with his feet. He played 16 times for England but, possibly, the greatest compliment to his fame was when almost 40,000 people attended his testimonial game, 25 years after he had retired from playing. On retirement he had several jobs including licensee of the Dublin Packet in Chester. The passionate atmosphere of a Goodison derby match provided the ironic and perhaps appropriate venue for the heart attack from which he died. In his career he totalled 379 league goals and his fame has provided a suitable nickname for subsequent generations of Deans.

DENNIS, Les

After serving his apprenticeship in the Merseyside clubs he began to receive national TV exposure as a result of appearances on the Russ Abbot shows, etc. He formed a highly promising and successful partnership with Dustin Gee, which tragically ended when Gee died from a heart attack whilst appearing at a pantomime in Southport at the beginning of 1986.

DERBY, Earls of

The Stanley family have lived at Knowsley since the 14th century when John de Stanley, grandfather of the 1st Earl of Derby, married Isabel Lathom. She was the heiress to vast estates in West Derby.

The family has a long, distinguished and interesting history. It was the 12th Earl who founded the world-famous Epsom horse race named after him in 1780, and he was still at Knowsley when Edward Lear was invited to draw the animals housed in one of Europe's best-known menageries.

The 14th Earl, born at Knowsley in 1799 was three times Prime Minister and the Conservative Party's longest-ever serving leader. The fifteenth Earl was Foreign Secretary under Disraeli, as well as serving under Gladstone when he joined the Liberal Party. The 17th Earl entered the Commons in 1892 and was Lord Roberts' Secretary during the Boer War, Postmaster General and Ambassador to Paris. He introduced the Derby scheme of recruitment for the Armed Services. He shared his family's love of horse racing and owned the Derby winners of 1924 (Sansovino) and 1933 (Hyperion) as well as six St. Leger winners. The 18th Earl, Edward John Stanley, born in 1918, served in the Grenadier Guards and was awarded a Military Cross in 1944. He has been President of the Merseyside Chamber of Commerce, Chancellor of Lancaster University, and President of the Rugby League.

DERBY HOUSE

(Exchange Flags) Known as the Citadel, here was located the Combined Headquarters, Western Approaches, during the Second World War, where the Battle of the Atlantic was organised against the German U-Boats. After America entered the war, their troops and supplies landed in Liverpool and, as well as helping the war effort, the G.I's were responsible for an increase in exports. Many of the girls they met left to start a new life in the U.S. with them. Many Merseyside girls met the men of their dreams, who were stationed at nearby Burtonwood.

Sir Max Kennedy Horton, the famous Admiral and quintessential war hero, was Commander-in-Chief, Western Approaches. The son of a member of the London Stock Exchange, he was born at the Maelog Lake Hotel, Rhosneigr, Anglesey. He was honoured with the highest decorations of USA, France, Holland and Norway. Liverpool awarded him the Freedom of the City and his state funeral was held at Liverpool Cathedral in 1951. A memorial was unveiled there in 1957.

DOBSON, Matthew

Liverpool physician who, in 1774 at his practice in Harrington Street, helped discover the link between sugar and diabetes.

DOCKERS' NAMES

Words are a form of currency in Liverpool and few have more wealth than the dockers. The Liverpool docker is often as articulate(d) as the lorry he is unloading.

This is perfectly illustrated in the "names" which dockers have bestowed upon their colleagues over the years.

Sam Goldwyn: "Let me put you in the picture".

The Sheriff (a foreman): "Where's the hold up?"

'Dixie' beats Bolton's Dick Pym to score the first goal of a hat-trick at Goodison on 29 December, 1928. Pym played in three FA Cup Finals without conceding a goal.

The 10.45 a.m. on time as usual.

Reluctant Plumber: "He won't do a tap".
The Spaceman: "Going to Ma's for dinner".
Wonder Boy: "I wonder what's in this?"
Lino: "He's always on the floor".
The Piano Man: "You're playing on me".
Phil the Cot: "Father of many".
Parish Priest: "Works every Sunday".
The Balloon Foreman: "Don't let me down, lads".
The Auctioneer: "Forklift driver who'd knock anything down".
The Daily Mirror: "I'll look into it".
The Baker: "Me and the tart".

DOCKERS' UMBRELLA

The Liverpool Overhead Railway — the world's first elevated electric railway — opened in 1893 and ran the length of the docks from Dingle to Seaforth Sands stopping at 15 stations en-route. It was also the first railway in the world to have an automatic signalling system and its elevated line provided a natural umbrella when the weather was less than clement. Over 11 million people used the railway in peak years. The last train ran on 30 December, 1956, and the railway was demolished in 1958.

DOD, Charlotte (Lottie)

Born 29 September 1871, Merseyside's and Britain's best-ever all-round sportswoman.
The daughter of a Liverpool cotton merchant, she was the youngest player to win the Ladies' Singles title at Wimbledon in 1887 when she was just 15. She won again in 1888, 1891, 1892, and 1893. She won the British Ladies' Golf Championship in 1904 at Troon and an Olympic Silver Medal for Archery at the 1908 London Olympiad. She also played hockey for her country.

DODD, Kenneth A.

Arguably Britain's best comedian was born in Knotty Ash, Liverpool, on 8 November, 1927, and has made that suburb of his home City nationally-known. A prolific joke-teller, he is the creator of a mythical comedy world of his own, filled with diddy men, tickling sticks, jam butty mines, et al. A former coalman and door-to-door salesman, he was educated at Holt High School, Childwall, and made his professional debut in 1954 at the Nottingham Empire. In the succeeding thirty years or so he has enjoyed tremendous success and popularity on the radio, TV, as a recording artist with many hit records, ("Tears" got to No.1 in 1965), and as Malvolio in 'Twelfth Night'. But it is on stage and with an audience that he especially excels. He has secured a place in the all-time comedy Hall of Fame, although still appears to have difficulty in finding his shirt. Devoted follower of Liverpool FC and Runcorn FC director.

DOOLEY, Arthur

Colourful and controversial sculptor with much evidence in Liverpool of his work and talent. The work 'Christ on the Cross' at Princes Road Methodist Church is particularly striking. Arthur, a former deckhand and Grenadier Guard, has been at the forefront when fighting for local causes close to his heart. In 1973. he was quoted in the Liverpool Echo as saying, "The great hope for the City is to develop the immense assets of the South Docks for light industry, housing and tourism".
Arthur, where are you now?

DURR, Frankie

Veteran Liverpool jockey who won the 2,000 Guineas in 1973

(Mon Fils) and 1978 (Roland Gardens) and the St. Leger in 1966 (Sodium) and 1973 (Peleid).

DUTTON, Joseph E.
1874-1905. Biologist, attended Liverpool University and travelled with Liverpool School of Tropical Medicine team to Africa to study mosquito and malaria link. Discovered, in Gambia, tryanosome in man which caused sleeping sickness, and the cause of tick fever (1904). Died of fever at Kosongo.

DYSON, Arnold

Arthur Dooley

Merseyside's Mr. Universe winner of 1953, three years after a rather more famous name, Steve Reeves.

Students from Knotty Ash University parade a replica of their Chancellor — Professor Dicky Mint . . . Panto Day procession, 1966.

E

ECHO and the BUNNYMEN
Contemporary Liverpool band enjoying large cult-following and commercial success since their first recording, "Pictures on My Wall", in 1979, culminating in their compilation album 'Songs to Learn and Sing' released late 1985. Started in the Liverpool bedroom of Will Sergeant when Ian McCulloch came over to experiment with his guitar.

EGERTON, Mary Ellen ("Ma")
Famous Liverpool publican who managed the American Bar and the Eagle (Ma Egerton's) behind the Empire. She had on her walls a collection of pictures of famous thespians. Dublin-born, she saw Crippen one evening in a London pub, and recognised jewellery on the lady he was with, as belonging to Belle Elmore, Crippen's wife who had been "missing" for some time. Her observation and subsequent calling of the police eventually led to Crippen's arrest and hanging.

ELLISON, Norman
Born in Waterloo in 1893, he was a natural history expert and wrote a popular column for the Liverpool Echo as "Nomad", between 1945-1963. He also broadcast 300 "Wandering with Nomad" radio programmes during those years.

The Bunnymen, 'Larks in the Park', Sefton Park, Liverpool 1982.

EDUCATING RITA
Smash-hit play by Willy Russell about a working class Liverpool girl's thirst for knowledge and intellectual advancement. The film of the play starred Michael Caine and Julie Walters. Also a poem by Roger McGough.

EE-AYE-ADDIO
Famous Kop chant of the sixties. The ritualist chanting, singing and swaying of the modern football crowd all began (in Britain) under the corrugated acoustic roof of the Kop. This sacred terrace, named after a hill in South Africa (Spion Kop) where soldiers of the Queen fought the Boer War, became the model for crowds all over the country as media teams arrived to document and chronicle this primitive phenomenom. In those days the Beatles may have been the world's most famous group, but the Kop made sure that it was the biggest and the loudest.

ELMES, Harvey Lonsdale
Precocious architect whose design for St. George's Hall was accepted in a competition when he was just 23 years of age. He didn't live to see the building completed and it was maintained that the stress he felt during the construction of the Hall contributed to his early death. He died in Jamaica, aged 33.

ENTENTE CORDIALE
A much earlier example of Anglo/French co-operation than Concorde or the Channel Tunnel happened on Merseyside in 1866. A Monsieur André of Paris and Mr. Hornblower of Liverpool won the competition to design Liverpool's Sefton Park, at that time 269 acres of treeless ground.

ENTIRE POPULATION OF CHINA

are from Liverpool. No, not a legacy of Liverpool's maritime and seafaring influence, but the name of a rock band headed by Janine Dawson. Pundits in the know are prophesying that they will be a big name of the future.

EPSTEIN, Brian

Following up Raymond Jones's enquiry — the customer who had asked for a Beatles record — Epstein left the family record store, Nems in Whitechapel, and walked the few yards to the dank, musky cellar club in Mathew Street to see and hear for himself. Perhaps the Beatles were too great not to be unearthed evenutally from their cellar full of noise, but it was Epstein who unearthed them, and as a result became the most successful pop manager of the Sixties. Born in Rodncy Street in 1935, he also managed Gerry and The Pacemakers, Billy J. Kramer, Cilla Black and others. He died aged 32, in August 1967, from an accidental overdose of drugs and alcohol.

ERICS

'Keep Eric's open' is the reason for this march in Liverpool in 1980. Even the policeman seems to agree.

Fashionable club which opened in 1976 as the Revolution, changing to Erics in May 1977 after the demise of the New Cavern Club, in Mathew Street. A new wave of Liverpool talent played the venue — China Crisis, Teardrop Explodes, Orchestral Manoeuvres in the Dark, Flock of Seagulls, Lotus Eaters, Echo and the Bunnymen, Frankie goes to Hollywood, and Peter Wylie and Wah.
The bands went on to national acclaim and some were responsible for much of the innovatory music of the late 1970's and 1980's, as well as top ten hits. Peter Wylie and Wah produced the album 'Word to the Wise Guy' in 1984, a

musical social document of their times. Flock of Seagulls won a prestigious Grammy Award in 1982 for best instrumental recording.

EVANS, Sir Charles

Deputy leader on the 1953 Everest-conquering expedition under John Hunt. A surgeon in Walton Hospital, Liverpool, he was an experienced Himalayan climber when chosen for the team that caught everybody's imagination. The news broke of their success, on the morning of Queen Elizabeth's Coronation on 2 June. He did not return with the party immediately, staying behind to prepare maps of the Everest region. He was knighted in 1969.

EVANS, Lord Horace

1903-1963. Physician, educated at Liverpool College. Son of Harry Evans (Liverpool musician) and Edith G. Evans. Physician to King George VI and Queen Mary and to Queen Elizabeth II from 1952. Created a Baron in 1957.

EVANS, Sir Hywel

Educated at Liverpool Collegiate and Liverpool University, he was appointed Chairman of the Welsh Arts Council in 1981.

EVANS, Robert

Born 28 May, 1927, and educated at Old Swan College, and Liverpool University, he was appointed Chief Executive, British Gas Corporation, in 1983.

EVERETT, Kenny

Kenny — in the best possible taste.

Perhaps to his chagrin was born on the 25 December, Maurice Cole, in the black and white Liverpool of 1944, a real Christmas present for his parents. He realised his technicolour dreams in the Beatle era and has since matured as one of Britain's most inventive entertainers on Radio and TV. Kenny has spent his professional life trying to escape from his reality and has succeeded, to the enjoyment and entertainment of his countless devotees.

EVERTON FC

One of the original member clubs of the Football League when it was formed in 1888, Everton FC have a long and proud history. "Nil Satis Nisis Optimum" is the club motto and over the years they have had many great teams and players. Founded in 1878 as St. Domingo's Sunday School, they moved to Anfield in 1884 and after a dispute over rent, moved to what is now Goodison Park in 1892. At that time they played in ruby shirts and it wasn't until the mid 1890's that they switched to the famous royal blue. Everton have aggregated more First Division points than any other club, and have won the championship on 8 occasions – in 1891, 1915, 1928, 1932, 1939, 1963, 1970 and 1985. The FA Cup was won in 1906, when Sandy Young scored the winning goal against Newcastle United, and again in 1933 when a glittering line up of star names defeated Manchester City 3-0. The club's third FA Cup victory was in 1966 when, after being two goals down to Sheffield Wednesday, they staged a famous comeback to win 3-2. A little known Cornishman, Mike Trebilcock, scored two goals that day and locally-born Derek Temple scored the winner. A fourth FA Cup win followed in 1984 when Watford were beaten 2-0.

The club has had many great players over the years — Makepeace, Sharp, Sagar, Cresswell, Britton, Geldard, Dunn, Mercer, Lawton and, the most famous of all, 'Dixie' Dean. In more recent years Vernon, West, Labone, Wilson, Ball, and the idolised Alex Young have worn the royal blue with distinction.

After spending the seventies and early eighties in the shadows of their neighbours and great rivals, the club has recently re-

The players' joy is obvious — Peter Reid is about to join the action, Andy Gray is ecstatic and Rapid Vienna are beaten in Rotterdam.

emerged and, in 1985, won the championship and gave a brilliant performance to defeat Rapid Vienna in the European Cup Winners Cup Final. They also reached the FA Cup Final and were voted Team of the Year. Players such as Southall (1985 Footballer of the Year), Ratcliffe, Steven and 1985 PFA Player of the Year, Peter Reid, are worthy successors to their illustrious predecessors.

The signing of Gary Lineker in 1985 proved to be an inspired one as he had a tremendous season scoring 40 goals and was voted Footballer of the Year. He was also one of four Everton players, with Reid, Stevens and Steven who were part of England's 1986 World Cup squad.

Lineker, with 6 goals, was the competition's top scorer. This helped to persuade Barcelona's Terry Venables to pay almost £3m for his signature.

Rotterdam, a Dutch Policeman becomes an Evertonian . . .

Kevin Ratcliffe with the 1985 championship trophy.

... and supporters play an impromptu match against a police team. As well as their team's superb performance in the Cup Winners Cup Final, the supporters proved great ambassadors for their club and the City.

Everton supporters at Euston Station on their way to the 1933 FA Cup Final.

EVERYMAN THEATRE

Started in 1964 by, among others, Terry Hands, now a director with the Royal Shakespeare Company. Early productions included Richard III, Look Back in Anger, The Importance of Being Earnest . . . indications of the company's range of output.

Several of Willy Russell's plays have premiered at the Theatre including in March 1986, "Shirley Valentine", much acclaimed study of "Liverpool Woman", played initially by Noreen Kershaw. The Theatre now enjoys a reputation as a significant breeding ground of British drama.

EVERY STREET

Situated off West Derby Road. Included as it accommodates well-known Liverpudlian boast "I know Every Street in Liverpool".

EUMORFOPOULOS, George

Distinguished collector of Chinese art, much of which has found its way into the country's museums. Born in Liverpool in 1863 of Greek parentage, he became Vice-president of Ralli Brothers, the cotton merchants. He died in 1939.

F

FAGAN, Joe

Emerged from the famous Boot Room to become Liverpool FC's first Liverpool-born manager in July, 1983, and the oldest newly-appointed manager in Football League history at 62.

In his first season he won the Manager of the Year award as his team achieved a unique treble — Championship, European Cup and Milk Cup. He announced his retirement prior to the tragic Brussels European final, a most unfitting end to the carer of a devoted and genial football man.

FAGIN, Joe

The "other Joe", chart topping local singer with "Thats Living All Right" from TVs "Auf Wiedersehn Pet".

FALK, Bernard

Brings a regular airing of wise Liverpudlian wit to Radio 4 as presenter of programmes such as 'Breakaway'.

FARRELL, J.G.

Novelist born in Liverpool in 1935, James Gordon Farrell wrote several bizarre and very funny novels. Troubles (1970) is set in a decaying Irish hotel and centres around a collection of eccentrics against a background of terrorism in the years 1919-1922. Other novels include: A Girl in the Head, The Siege of Krishnapur (1973 Booker Prize Winner) and the Singapore Grip. He lived alone in a farmhouse in West Cork and was drowned in 1979.

FARRELL, Tom

The Liverpool Harrier who was United Kingdom 400 metres hurdles record holder, running 51.10 seconds in 1957, and who represented his country many times including at the 1956 and 1960 Olympics. He captained the British team at the European Championships in 1958. He taught at several schools on Merseyside, including Quarry Bank, before being ordained in 1971.

FERRANTI, Sebastian Ziani de

Born in Bold Street, Liverpool, in 1864. Electrical engineer and inventor (he took out 176 patents). Planned electric supply station at Deptford which supplied all of London, north of the Thames.

Pioneer of high voltage systems and long distance transmission of high voltage electricity. He started Ferranti Ltd. at Oldham in 1896, was made a Fellow of the Royal Society in 1927 and died, at Zurich, in 1930.

Liverpool had a strong link with another famous electrical engineer, Henry Royce, the co-founder of the famous motor car firm, when he was invited to be Chief Engineer for a pioneer scheme of street lighting in Liverpool in 1882.

FIRSTS

Many of Liverpool's firsts are recorded elsewhere in this book and it would need a complete book to do them all justice. However, they include:

The World's first School for the Blind — 1791.
The World's first Public Washhouse — 1842.

On the way to the wash-house in Picton Road is Mrs Mary Coyne.

The World's first Medical Officer of Health —
Dr W. H. Duncan.
The first disarmament campaign, organised by Liverpool Peace Society in 1875.
The first railway timetable (Lacy's) — 1835.
The first British School of Architecture — 1895.
The first steamroller in Britain was purchased by Liverpool City Council in 1867.
John Hope of Liverpool fitted a mileometer in a car, the first in the country.
The first motorised British fire engine was built in Liverpool and used by Liverpool Fire Service in 1901.
Liverpool organisations were forerunners of the R.S.P.C.A. and N.S.P.C.C. and Liverpool's docks were the first commercial dock system in the world.

FLAG DAYS
The first Flag Day in Britain was held in Liverpool in 1913.

FLEMYNG, Robert
Veteran stage, film, and TV actor, born in Liverpool in 1912, he was awarded a Military Cross during the Second World War. Spent three years at the Playhouse in the early 1930's. His film credits include: "The Blue Lamp", "The Man who Never Was", The Holly and the Ivy", and on TV: "Compact" and "Family Solicitor".
He was awarded an O.B.E.

Robert Flemyng

FOOTBALL SUPPORTERS ASSOCIATION
Launched in Liverpool, the brainchild of Rogan Taylor and Peter Garrett, and pledged to restore soccer to the fans and honour to the terraces. Its first public meeting was held in London at County Hall on Monday, 27 January, 1986.

FOOTBALL CHALLENGE
From the many locally-born footballers there are infinite permutations of English representative sides, unless the Republic of Ireland get them first! The authors have selected two a current England team versus an Old England team (post-war).

Current England XI

Martin Hodge
Sheffield Wednesday

John Gidman
Man. City

Alvin Martin
West Ham

Dave Watson
Everton

John Bailey
Newcastle Utd

Mark Ward
West Ham

Peter Reid
Everton

Steve McMahon
Liverpool

John Aldridge
Oxford Utd

Peter Withe
Sheffield Utd

Peter Davenport
Manchester Utd

Referee: Bill Evans *Liverpool*

JACK SHARP

David Johnson
Everton, Ipswich, Liverpool

Joe Baker
Hibernian

Steve Coppell
Man. Utd

Colin Harvey
Everton

Denis Mortimer
Aston Villa

Terry McDermott
Newcastle & Liverpool

Gerry Byrne
Liverpool

Brian Labone
Everton

Roy McFarland
Derby Co.

Chris Lawler
Liverpool

Stan Hanson
Bolton

Old England XI (Post-War)

Managers to be appointed from:
Stan Cullis, Joe Mercer, Joe Fagan, Ron Atkinson, Ron Saunders, Bobby Campbell, Jimmy Melia, Steve Coppell, Len Ashurst, Mick Lyons, Joe Royle, Harry Storer, Jnr.,

Current England XI Reserves: Jimmy Rimmer *(Man. Utd. Swansea, A. Villa),* Derek Mountfield *(Everton),* Jimmy Case *(Southampton),* Phil Thompson *(Liverpool),* Billy Wright *(Birmingham City),* Ian Bowyer *(Notts Forest),* Mike Lyons *(Grimsby),* Howard Gayle *(Sunderland),* Tommy Caton *(Arsenal),* Sammy Lee *(Q.P.R.).*

Old England XI Reserves: Fred Davies *(Wolves),* Albert Dunlop *(Everton),* Harry Leyland *(Everton),* Bill Jones *(Liverpool),* Laurie Hughes *(Liverpool),* Tommy Wright *(Everton),* Jimmy Payne *(Liverpool),* Jimmy Dugdale *(A. Villa, WBA),* Jimmy Melia *(Liverpool),* John McAlle *(Wolves),* Les Shannon *(Burnley),* Bill Eckersley *(Blackburn),* Alan A'Court *(Liverpool),* Dave Hickson *(Everton),* Len Ashurst *(Sunderland),* Willie Carlin *(Derby Co.)* Johnny Morrissey *(Everton),* Tony Coleman *(Man. City),* Derek Temple *(Everton),* Jimmy Harris *(Everton),* George Burnett *(Everton).*

A balcony in Queen's Drive provides a vantage point for this celebration of soccer support.

No its not 'Pongo' Waring, Rover of the Rovers or even Norman 'bites yer legs' Hunter, but he is a real terrier in the tackle. His favourite ground is Kennelworth Road where he's often given his team the lead. Good at picking up scraps in the penalty area he loved playing against Peter 'the Cat' Boneti but hates playing Wolves. A rabid fan of Alan Rough Rough the Scottish international goalkeeper and Liverpool's John Warkies and their great Dane Jan Molby. Trouble at matches makes this dog Spit and he was once substituted at half time because his manager Kenny Dogleash described him as being . . . dog-tired. Signed from Rexham for Liverpool which was a bone of contention with Howard Kennel. Now lives at Wavertree.

The Frankies pictured at the rock event of 1986 — 'Rock around the Albert Dock'.

FOOT, Michael

The former leader of the Labour Party was converted to Socialism during his working stay in Liverpool in the 1930's. During his period in the City he wrote the following words of poetry, his first published work, which serves as a reminder to elderly Evertonians of halcyon days of the 1930's:
"When at the call my weary feet I turn,
The gates of paradise are opened wide.
At Goodison I know a man may learn,
Rapture more rich than Anfield can provide,
In Coulter's skill and Geldard's subtle speed,
I see displayed in all its matchless bounty,
The power of which the heavens themselves decreed,
The fall of Sunderland and Derby County
The hands of Sagar, Dixie's priceless head
Made smooth the path to Wembley till that day
When Bolton came. Now hopes are fled
And all is sunk in bottomless dismay ?
And so I watch with heart and temper cool,
God's lesser breed of men at Liverpool.

FORD MOTORS FC

The only Merseyside football team to play in Europe during the ill-fated 1985/86 season. Winners of the Ford European Cup in 1985, the first round of the 85/86 competition saw them drawn against an Italian team in the aftermath of Brussels. However, the Italians said they had never played against friendlier people and really enjoyed themselves. This, despite Ford of Halewood winning 7-0.

FORRESTER, Helen

Hoylake-born author who has recounted her poverty-stricken childhood days in Liverpool in Two Pence to Cross the Mersey" a best seller with several sequels. A radio adaptation was broadcast on BBC Radio 4 in April 1986.

Billy Fury at Epsom. His horse, Anselmo, was fourth in the 1964 Derby.

FRANCES, Frank Sir

Born in Liverpool and educated at Liverpool Institute. Director and Principal Librarian, British Museum, 1958-1969.

FRANKIE GOES TO HOLLYWOOD

So said the headline (referring to Sinatra) and that seemed a good name for this controversial Liverpool band, who in 1984 equalled their fellow Townies (Gerry and the Pacemakers) record by reaching No.1 in the charts with their first three released recordings. Led by Holly Johnson, their first record, "Relax", was banned by the BBC but was a world-wide hit record and tee-shirt.

The groups album entitled 'Liverpool' was released in Autumn, 1986.

FREEMAN, Gyn

A leading presenter of BBC's Radio West Midlands, large and loveable Liverpudlian who delights her Midland audience.

FURY, Billy

Liverpool's and Britain's 'Elvis' was born Ronnie Wycherley and at one time worked on the Mersey tugboats. Signed by Larry Parnes after the impressario had seen him performing at a Birkenhead rock concert, Fury went on to be a regular hit performer and to develop a sensual, moody style which epitomised the early rock age. His classic "Halfway to Paradise" has become one of the great golden oldies. His life-long struggle against heart trouble finally ended in 1983 when he died, aged 42.

FYFE, David Patrick Maxwell — Lord Kilmuir

1900-1967. Conservative MP for Liverpool West Derby 1935-1954. He was in chambers in Liverpool with Sir George Lynskey and a leading barrister in Merseyside's legal history of the 1930's.

He was Deputy Chief Prosecutor at the Nuremberg Trials, Home Secretary, Lord Chancellor, Solicitor-General. Chairman of Plesseys. Harold McMillan dropped him from his Cabinet in 1962 and he then accepted an earldom.

43

G

GADD, Reg
Of Sunlight Street, Liverpool 5. A prolific writer of featured letters in the 'Liverpool Echo' during the sixties and seventies, mostly about soccer and boxing topics.

GAMLIN, Lionel
Birkenhead-born radio announcer, presenter and producer. He conducted interviews on "In Town Tonight" and was a straight man to Old Mother Riley. In 1949 he devised and presented "Hello, Children" (later "Hello There"), a popular children's magazine programme which was broadcast on the Light Programme during school holidays until 1953.

GARDEN FESTIVAL
The United Kingdom's first International Garden Festival was held in Liverpool in 1984. Situated on a 250 acres' site at Riverside to the south of the City Centre — an area known to Liverpudlians as the "Cast Iron Shore", or "The Cazzie". The area was revitalised in a remarkably short period of time, to be transformed into a wonderland of exhibits from 28 countries.

The Merseyside Development Corporation, led by Chairman Leslie C. Young, were responsible for this vast project and the Festival exceeded its objectives and attracted more than the hoped-for 3 million visitors, and was Britain's most successful tourist attraction of 1984. The site, with many of the original amenities retained, offers tremendous potential and a great attraction for locals and tourists alike.

GARRICK, David

Liverpudlian pop singer who had trained for the opera. Had minor hits in 1966 'Lady Jane' and 'Dear Mrs Applebee' but his backing group went on to have 3 Top Ten hits in 1970-72 as Badfinger.

Badfinger group member, Liverpool-born Tom Evans, was co-writer of "Without You" a world-wide hit and No.1 in Britain for Harry Nillson in 1972.

GASKIN, Prof. Maxwell

Born in 1921, educated at Quarry Bank and Liverpool University, he was awarded the DFC and Bar for his service in RAF Bomber Command. Now a professor at Aberdeen University and author of several books, including a number on the effects of the new Scottish economy.

GARVIN, James Louis

(1868-1947). The great editor of 'The Observer' (1908-1942) was born in Birkenhead and educated at Park Street School. The son of an Irish immigrant, his father was lost at sea when Garvin was two. He was responsible for the development of the Observer's format of in-depth news and arts coverage. He also edited the 14th edition of Encyclopaedia Brittanica in 1929. He declined a Knighthood from Lloyd George but accepted a Companion of Honour.

GEAR, The

Scouse joy.

GLADSTONE, William Ewart

Born at 62 Rodney Street in 1809, he was the greatest British reforming statesman of the 19th century. He became leader

of the Liberal Party in 1866 and Prime Minister for the first time in 1868. During his first administration he reformed the legal system, education, and the Army, passed the Irish Land Act and established secret ballots and elections. He had further terms as Prime Minister between 1880-85, 1886, and 1892-94 but never achieved his plans for Irish Home Rule. A great orator, his political beliefs were founded upon strong religious convictions.

He was buried at Westminster Abbey and there is a monument in his honour in St. John's Gardens. The famous red Gladstone case is still a part of Budget Day tradition and Queen Victoria once said of him; "He talks to me as though I were a public meeting".

GOALKEEPER

Liverpool's FC's telegraphic address. The Club has had many famous international keepers: Scott, Campbell, Hardy, Sidlow, Clemence. As far as can be established the current Zimbabwean international, Grobbelaar, is the only one who actually walked on his hands.

GOLF

The Royal Liverpool Club at Hoylake has played a significant role in the development of the game. Founded in 1869 and one of the earliest seaside links in England, it was the venue of the first British Amateur Championships in 1885, the following year the competition was taken over by the R. & A. The first English Amateur championship was held here, as well as the first matches between England and Scotland and Great Britain and the USA. In 1902 the club provided six players out of 20 in the Scotland and Ireland match. The first British "Open" to be held at Hoylake was in 1897, won by a member, and among famous Hoylake 'Open' winners were Bobby Jones (1930) Fred Daly (1947) Peter Thomson (1956) and the Argentinian Roberto de Vicenzo in 1967, a win which produced stirring and emotional scenes as the popular 44-year old walked down the eighteenth.

Hoylake's 1967 Open Winner.

The Liverpool club has had its Royal prefix since 1872. The Royal Birkdale club near Southport has been the venue of many major championships since hosting its first 'Open' in 1954 (Peter Thomson the winner).

The Ryder Cup match held there in 1969 resulted in a tie. The Formby Club founded in 1884 inaugurated a Ladies' Section in 1896 and is one of the few courses with an entirely separate ladies' course. The dunes of the Hillside Club were used for the filming of the Desert Song, the famous silent film of the 1920s and the Stableford scoring system was introduced by a member of the Wallasey Club, Dr. Frank Stableford. One of the world's earliest forms of golf trolley was introduced at the Leasowe Club in 1937. The Wirral Ladies Golf Club established in 1894 — unique in Europe as it was owned and run entirely by its lady members.

GOODISON PARK
Home of Everton FC and one of the most famous football grounds in the country. Over 78,000 fans attended the immediate post-war games before the ground was modernised and the capacity reduced. As one of the grounds used for the 1966 World Cup, it staged the competition's greatest match, Hungary 3-Brazil 1, when, on a wet and windy night, over 50,000 Merseysiders chanted the name of the Hungarian centre forward "Albert, Albert" who played brilliantly. They could have named a dock after him that night.
The venue of England's first-ever home defeat by other than a British team in 1949 — the Republic of Ireland captained by Everton's Peter Farrell won 2-0. The 1894 FA Cup Final was played at the ground, as was the 1910 Final replay.

GRAFTON ROOMS, The
West Derby Road. Perhaps the City's best known dance hall. The venue of a high percentage of first meetings for Mr. and Mrs. Liverpool.
The long-running Monday over-30's night gave the hall the rather unkind name of the "elephants' burial ground".

GREAT EASTERN
One of the most famous of ships, the largest steamship of its day when launched in 1858, designed by Brunel. One hundred years ago at the end of its life, it was used by Lewis's as an exhibition ship. It's mast is the flagpole at the Kop end of Liverpool FC's Anfield ground.

GREAT GEORGE
The Liver Clock, so called because it was started the moment King George V was crowned on 22 June, 1911. Bigger than Big Ben — the biggest in England, in fact, it has four dials; the diameter of each dial is 25 feet, and is located on Liverpool's best known international symbol, the Royal Liver Building.

GREENWOOD, Debbie
The lovely Liverpool judy who beat three other lovely Liverpool judies (amongst others) to the 1984 Miss Great Britain title. A former Breakfast TV presenter and quiz show hostess.

GREGSON, John
Popular "nice guy" film actor born in Liverpool, 1919, who appeared in many of the British cinema's successful early post war films. These included "Genevieve", "Battle of the River Plate" and "Miracle in Soho". He died in 1975.

GREGSON, Matthew
1749-1824. Local man, member of famous shipbuilding family, he refused a knighthood. Producer of a famous early book on antiquities "Fragments".

GUYLER, Deryck

Born in Wallasey in 1914 and educated at Liverpool College, this veteran character actor initially made his name on radio's "ITMA", particularly as Frisby Dyke. Among his countless other roles include Inspector Scott in "Inspector Scott Investigates" which ran for 7 series on radio from July 1957 until 1963. He was P.C. 'Corky' Turnbull in the popular Eric Sykes' TV programmes.

GEORGE GREEN *The Liverpool Echo's famed football cartoonist. This is the 1933 FA Cup Final offering (the first Final in which the players were numbered).*

H

Johnny Hackett with the man who persuaded him to turn professional — Liverpool comic Jimmy Couton and dog, Rex.

HACKETT, Johnny
Popular Liverpool-born comedian who resembles French comedy 'great', Fernandel . . . facially.

HADDEN, Rev. Robert Henry
1854-1909. Liverpool-born, honorary chaplain to Queen Victoria and King Edward VII. Educated at Merchant Taylor's, Crosby, and the son of a proprietor of the Liverpool Courier.
Times correspondent, President of the Oxford Union and author.

HALF MAN, HALF BISCUIT
Birkenhead band whose 1986 LP 'Back in the D.H.S.S.' included a number of extravagantly titled gems such as "I hate Nerys Hughes from the Heart, and "I Love you because you look like Jim Reeves". The album was recorded by Messrs. Crossley Wright, Lloyd and the two Blackwells at Vulcan Studios, Waterloo, but didn't include their earlier single contribution, "All I want for Christmas is the Dukla Prague away kit". A Subbuteo lovers' plea from the heart?
Tranmere Rovers fanatics, they turned down the opportunity to appear on TV's 'The Tube' in favour of watching Rovers play Scunthorpe United.

HALL, Sir William Reginald
Famous naval Admiral who was Unionist MP for Liverpool West Derby between 1919-1923. He introduced the three-watch system to the Navy and was responsible for deciphering German naval messages during the First World War as Director, Intelligence Division. He was also instrumental in the capture of Roger Casement. He was known as 'Blinker' for his habit of blinking rapidly when talking.

HALLIDAY, Edward Irvine
Born in the same street as union leader Jack Jones — York Street, Garston — but 11 years earlier, in 1902. A distinguished painter who was President of the Royal Society of Portrait Painters. Educated at Liverpool Institute, Liverpool College and Liverpool College of Art, he has painted portraits of the Queen, Queen Mother, Earl Mountbatten and other members of the Royal Family as well as Nehru, Kenneth Kaunda, King Olaf and Sir Edmund Hillary.

HAMILTON, Russ
Liverpool singer, born Ronnie Hulme in Everton, and former Butlins' Red Coat who was the first British artist to achieve a gold disc in America, for "Rainbow", in 1957. His hit record "We Will Make Love" reached No. 2 in the British charts in 1957.

HANDLEY, Tommy and ITMA
Britain's greatest radio comedian was born in Trelfall Street, Liverpool 8, on 12 January, 1896. He made his first professional appearance at Daly's Theatre in 1917 in a production of "Maid of the Mountains" in the chorus line. He played the Halls and appeared on the radio, but it was the radio show "ITMA" that made him a national figure. The show had massive weekly audiences throughout the war and beyond, when millions of people tuned in for their morale to be raised by Handley's comic genius. He performed at a special show at Windsor Castle in 1942 on the occasion of the Queen's (then Princess Elizabeth) sixteenth birthday. ITMA lasted ten years until Handley's death in 1949, aged 52. Memorial services were held in Liverpool and St. Paul's cathedrals. In London, an estimated 10,000 people followed the service outside St. Paul's, listening to the proceedings from specially installed loudspeakers. He was once reported as ordering from the receptionist at the Adelphi Hotel, "The Jewish Chronicle and a bacon butty" with his early morning call.

Tommy Handley

ITMA

"It's That Man Again" was a significant landmark in British broadcasting. Ted Kavanagh, with the help of Tommy Handley, wrote the show which was first broadcast in July 1939. Much of Handley's comic inventiveness stemmed from his observations of Liverpool life and its characters. Frisby Dyke, the famous Scouse character, was the name of a draper's shop in Liverpool. Poppy Poopart and Peter Geekie were also Liverpool trade names. The show produced a string of popular characters and catchphrases, some of which are still used today — "Can I do yer now, sir?" (Mrs. Mopp); "I don't mind if I do" (Colonel Chinstrap); "This is Funf speaking" (Funf); "It's being so cheerful as keeps me going" (Mona Lott); "Well I'll go to the foot of our stairs" (Handley himself); "Vicky Verky" (Norman) and "After you, Claude, No, after you, Cecil ; I waited for hours in a fish queue and this chap took my plaice". Other characters included Ruby Rockcake, Ali Oop, George Gorge, Sophie Tuckshop, Sam Scram, Sam Fairfechan and Tattie McIntosh. Among the personnel who played them were Merseyside's Deryck Guyler (who played Frisby Dyke), Jack Train, Molly Weir, Maurice Denham, Hattie Jacques, Hugh Morton, Fred Yule, Carleton Hobbs, Horace Percival, Joan Harben and Dorothy Summers as Mrs. Mopp.

Another of the show's catchphrases 'Don't forget the Diver' was devised by Handley as a result of a well-known one-legged character who used to dive into the Mersey at New Brighton on the arrival of the Liverpool ferry. As the passengers came down the gangway at the commencement of his performance, he would shout "Don't forget the diver, please give generously". The last programme was broadcast in January 1949. Three days later, on 9 January, Handley was dead and Britain's most-famed radio comedy show died with him.

HANNAH, George

Liverpool-born footballer of the 1950's. Can you find another player who scored a goal in an FA Cup Final for the winning team whose surname is a palindrome? The goal was for Newcastle United against Manchester City in 1955.

HARRISON, George

The youngest member of the Beatles and the first to have a solo No.1 Hit, "My Sweet Lord", in 1971. He was born at 12 Arnold Grove, Wavertree, in 1943. After playing for a while with the Les Stewart Quartet, he played for the first time with the Quarrymen at the Casbah Coffee Club in Haymans Green in August 1958. At the height of Beatlemania, George was the quiet one in the middle, but a talented guitarist who wrote amongst others the beautiful ballad, "Something". He married Patti Boyd, a model, in January 1966 (later disolved) and was instrumental in organising the concert for Bangladesh — a huge indoor rock concert held at Madison Square Gardens, New York, on 1 August, 1971, to raise funds for destitute Bangladeshis. Harrison, now actively involved in the production of British films, received a special 'Standard' film award for Handmade's contribution in 1986.

HARRISON, George

Liverpool Echo columnist who for many years wrote popular 'Over The Mersey Wall' column, and accompanied the Beatles on their first U.S. tour in 1964.

HARRISON, Rex

Somewhat surprisingly, this archetypal of the suave debonair, unflappable Englishman is, in fact, a Liverpudlian. Well he *was* born and educated in Liverpool. Attended Liverpool College and his early acting career was spent at the Playhouse. Star of countless movies, but will mostly be remembered for his role as Professor Higgins in "My Fair Lady", for which he won an Oscar in 1964, and as "Dr. Dolittle". Has a reputation for abrasiveness off the screen and has the nickname, "Sexy Rexy". However, an actor of exquisite timing and style.

HARRISON, Rob

Liverpool middle distance runner who has represented his country many times, and who won the 1985 European Indoor 800 metres title and the AAA's Indoor 1986 1500 metre title.

HARRY, Bill

Beatle expert and editor of Mersey Beat when the group were attaining initial local stardom. Attended Liverpool College of Art with John Lennon and is now an independent PR man in the music industry having represented such acts as Bowie, Pink Floyd, Hollies, Kinks, Kim Wilde and Hot Chocolate.

HARVEY, Colin
Liverpool-born right-hand man to Howard Kendall, who has played his part in Everton's stunning success of recent seasons. He was a cultured wing-half unlucky not to gain more than one England cap (against Malta, 1971). With Kendall and Alan Ball, he formed one of British football's most notable midfields, winning a Championship Medal in 1970 and an FA Cup Winner's Medal in 1966.

HATTON, Derek
Controversial deputy leader of Liverpool City Council, he became nationally known in 1985 in waging war with the Government over "cuts in services". He is a supporter of Everton FC, but don't Everton play in blue?

HATTON, John Liptrot
Composer, pianist and singer of a multitude of comic songs. Liverpool-born, he composed much of the music for Charles Kean's London productions. He toured Europe and the U.S.A. and his best-known songs "Simon the Cellarer" and "Oh, Anthea" are still popular.

HAWTHORNE, Nathaniel
1804-64. Considered to be one of America's greatest writers by many critics, he was U.S. Consul in Liverpool between 1853-57 and described Eastham 'across the water' as his favourite village. He lived at 26 Rock Park, Rock Ferry.

HAYGARTH, Tony
Liverpool born actor who had a major role in world wide TV hit, "Holocaust", and played Fidel Sanchez in ITV's 1986 series, "Farrington of the F.O". He was a colleague of Geoffrey Hughes at the Merseyside Unity Theatre.

HEATHCLIFFE
Fictional character from "Wuthering Heights". The gypsy boy was found wandering the streets of Liverpool before his emigration to the dark, brooding moors of Bronte's Yorkshire. Based on real life circumstances.

HEENAN, Cardinal
Much respected Archbishop of Liverpool between 1957-1963, when the City's Orange and Green factions were less tolerant, and a leading protagonist in the revised plans for the Metropolitan Cathedral. Became Archbishop of Westminster in 1963 until his death in November 1975.

HEFFER, Eric
Lively and "lovable" Labour MP who represents Liverpool Walton constituency and occasionally walks out of Labour Party Conferences. A former City councillor, he married à Liverpool girl and is pleased to be known as an honorary Scouse.

HEILBRON, Hon. Dame Rose
One of the two lady Kings Counsellors, Britain's first, appointed in 1949 and the first woman Recorder (Burnley 1956), she was Britain's second woman High Court Judge. Born in Liverpool 19 August, 1914 and educated at Belvedere School and Liverpool University where she gained a First Class Honours Degree. She was called to the Bar at Grays in 1939 and the first woman barrister to lead in a murder trial, the Cameo Cinema murder in Liverpool in 1949. George

Rose Heilbron

Kelly whom she was defending was reported as commenting "I don't want no judy defending me".

HEMANS, Felicia D
neé Browne, 1793-1835. Poetess, born at 118 Duke Street, Liverpool, wrote extremely popular sentimental verse. Her best known work, "Casabianca", contains arguably the most-quoted line in English poetry, "The boy stood on the burning deck".

HENDERSON'S
On a hot, sunny day in June 1960 eleven people perished in the worst Merseyside fire since the Blitz. The scene was the dignified Church Street store that William Henderson had opened in 1828 and Harrods had bought in 1949. The fire, which started on a busy weekday afternoon, only raged for just over an hour and, as well as the loss of life, caused severe damage to the building. The disaster produced its heroes. Among them were Colin Murphy, a ventilation engineer, who, realising the air-conditioning fans were helping to spread the fire, made an attempt to turn them off. Bill Terry, the Maintenance Manager, kept the flames at bay with a portable fire extinguisher, whilst the staff made their way out of the building. Both men died in the blaze. The store was rebuilt and reopened in 1962, and changes of ownership resulted in the name change to Binn's in 1976. It closed in 1983.

HENRI, Adrian
One man culture club, poet, painter, singer, songwriter, playwright, et al. His association with Roger McGough and Brian Patten was responsible for the emergence of the verbal Liverpool Sound of the Sixties, culminating in the tremendous success of their volume of poetry, "The Mersey Sound", which has sold in excess of 250,000 copies.

HER BENNY
A classic story of Victorian life in Liverpool written by Silas K. Hocking in 1879, who, for a time, was a clergyman in the City.

HIGSONS BREWERY
Liverpool's oldest brewery, established in 1780. "Higgies" has long been a feature of Mersey life. In recent years the company has created a generation of mythical Mersey characters — Lord Street, Ann Field, Clayton Square, Phil O'Monic, Pierre Head, etc. illustrated on beer mats. Now Liverpudlian collectors' items.

HILTON, Harold
The first player and the only Briton to have held the American and British amateur golf titles, at the same time (in 1911). A member of the Royal Liverpool Club, he won the first British Open to be held at Hoylake in 1897 following his first 'Open' success in 1892 at Muirhead.

HILLSIDERS
One of Britain's top country and western bands for many years, this Liverpool group are one of the few UK bands able to compete in this most American of musical styles.

HITCHMOUGH, Jim
Playwright from Knotty Ash whose debutant play "Watching" transferred from the Playhouse to London in 1986. Set in the Wirral, it starred Adam Kotz and Cheryl Maiker. Cheryl Maiker, together with Tony Carney, a product of the Everyman Youth Theatre, were the Scouse children of Hazel O'Connor in the BBC TV series, "Fighting Back", shown in 1986.

HOLLIDAY, Michael
Crosby (Bing) influenced ballad singer. Liverpool's nice guy crooner had tremendous success with hit records such as, "Story of My Life" (1958) and "Starry Eyed" (1960) which both got to No.1 in the charts. His sad death ended a career enjoyed by millions.

Michael Holliday, the singing voice of Sheriff Tex Tucker in the ITV series, 'Four Feather Falls'.

HOLY LAND
Nickname for Liverpool 8 district containing the streets of Moses, Isaac, Jacob, etc. Its survival from redevelopment suggests that the planners may consider it hallowed ground.

HOOKS, Linda
Model/actress born in Liverpool 1952 and educated at Childwall Valley High School. She won Miss Variety Club of Great Britain and Miss International (Tokyo) in 1972 and went on to appear in films and on TV (Sale of The Century, Celebrity Squares, The Sweeney, etc.)

HORNBY, Clive
Former drummer with the Dennisons, Mersey pop group of the 1960's, who had minor hits with "Be My Girl" (1963) and "Walkin' the Dog" (1964). Liverpool-born Clive went on to achieve national recognition playing Jack Sugden in Yorkshire TV's long running serial, "Emmerdale Farm".

HORROCKS, Jeremiah
Astronomer, born in Aigburth, Liverpool. In 1639 he was the first in the world to observe the passing of Venus across the sun, thus enabling the earth's distance from the sun to be calculated. His undoubted genius was not allowed to be fulfilled as he died, aged 23, in 1641.
Horrocks Avenue in Garston is named after him.

Rita Hunter after receiving her Honorary Degree of Doctor of Music at Liverpool University in 1983.

HOSPITAL RADIO
The first hospital radio network started in Liverpool in 1952.

HOWELL, Rob
Believed to be the only Romany to play soccer for England, he was on Liverpool's books in 1899 when he played against Scotland.
"It's just the gypsy in my goal"

HUGHES, Emlyn
Former Liverpool and England captain affectionately known as "Crazy Horse". He picked up silver more often in his career than did the "Lone Ranger". Footballer of the Year in 1977, he led Liverpool to many of their triumphs during the glory years of the 1970's. His life has been featured in Eamonn Andrew's famous red book and has appeared in several series of BBC's "Question of Sport".

HUGHES, Geoffrey
His portrayal of Eddie Yates in "Coronation Street" made him nationally known, although his thick Scouse accent may have limited the amount of dialogue he was given! He left the series in 1983. Will he ever return to the Rovers?

HUGHES, Ken
Film director/screenwriter. Born in Liverpool in 1922. He worked as a projectionist in a local cinema before moving to the BBC as an engineer. Amongst the 25-or-so films he has directed are "Joe Macbeth (well worth seeing with lovely Ruth Roman), "The Trials of Oscar Wilde", "In the Nick", "Jazzboat", "Chitty Chitty Bang Bang", and "Cromwell".

His 1963 film "The Small World of Sammy Lee" had nothing to do with the Liverpool-born footballer.

HUNT, Roger
Merseyside soccer star who played during Liverpool FC's successful years during the 1960's and nicknamed 'Sir Roger' by the Kop. Scored 41 goals in the 1961/62 promotion season. Born at Golborne, he played 34 times for England (18 goals) including the 1966 World Cup Final against West Germany. Perhaps the finest goal he scored was a dazzling volley against Herrera's Inter Milan in the European Cup Semi-Final, 1st Leg, at Anfield in May 1965. He remains the club's record goalscorer with 245 goals and is a member of the pools panel. A capacity crowd of 56,214 attended his testimonial match at Anfield on 11 April, 1972.

HUNTER, Rita
Merseyside prima donna with built in acoustics. Although leading soprano at Covent Garden since 1958, Rita has excelled in all of the famous opera houses throughout the world and now enjoys international acclaim. Born in Wallasey in 1933, and educated at Liscard Secondary Modern School (formerly Manor Road School), she trained under Eva Turner amongst others, and has played most of the leading roles, Brunhilde, Donna Anna, Elsa, etc. Now resident in Australia, she toured Britain in 1986, appeared on 'Wogan' and published her autobiography.

HUSKISSON, William
Liverpool MP who played a significant role in the establishment of the world's first major passenger railway between Liverpool and Manchester. With great irony, he was killed by the train on its opening day, 15 September, 1830. He was the founder of the Liverpool Institute School, "The Inny", in 1825.

HUTCHINSON, William
A Liverpool mariner whose invention of reflecting mirrors for lighthouses led to the first one in the world being built at Bidston, incorporating his invention in 1771.

I

IRVING, Washington
1783-1859. Famous American author and creator of 'Rip van Winkle'. He came to Liverpool to work as a merchant in 1817. He went bankrupt — which was a lot harder to do at the height of Liverpool's trading greatness.

ISLE OF MAN
Merseyside playground 60 miles away in the Irish Sea. A useful venue for local football teams prepared to test their prowess against Manx teams, many of whose players have three legs but, fortunately, no tails. One Manxman who came to Merseyside to seek his fortune was Costain who started the famous construction company in Waterloo in 1865.

J

Glenda, her Mum's sideboard and a few glittering prizes.

Birkenhead-born and the best thing ever to come out of Boots (she worked at the Hoylake branch of the famous chemists at one time). The only British woman to win Best Actress 'Oscars' twice, for 'Women in Love', in 1970, and 'A Touch of Class' in 1973. She was also nominated for her performance in John Schlesinger's 'Sunday, Bloody Sunday' in 1971. Her formidable talent has been demonstrated in a wide range of roles on stage, TV and films, from the time she gained her first major success in Peter Weiss's play, later filmed in 1964. The Title? The Persecution and Assassination of Jean-Paul Marat as performed by the inmates of the Asylum of Charenton under the direction of the Marquis de Sade.

JACKSON, Michael
No, not *the* Michael Jackson. Liverpool's was educated at Holt High School and after starting his acting career in rep. has appeared on TV in "Man About the House", "Hazell", "Crown Court", etc. Was voted "London Evening News Most Promising Newcomer" in 1978 for his role in "Sweeney 2".

JACQUES, Brian
Former docker, poet, broadcaster, artist, storyteller, comedian, folk singer with "The Fisherman". A sort of typical Scouse, really.

JACQUI & BRIDIE
A spin off from the Spinners, Jacqui McDonald and Bridie McDonnell established themselves in the British folk scene with their particular brand of ballad singing and writing.

JAMBOREE
The first ever World Scout Jamboree was held in Birkenhead's Arrowe Park, the Rally ground, in 1929 when some 50,000 scouts from over 70 countries attended. The Jamboree was held to celebrate 21 years of the Boy Scout movement founded by Baden Powell. His idea of the Scout movement had been first mentioned at the old YMCA building in Grange Road, Birkenhead on 24 January, 1908. A plaque recording this event is on the wall of the YMCA building in Whetstone Lane, Birkenhead.

Sir Alfred Pickford, the Camp Commissioner, inspects a stuffed cheetah exhibited by Singhalese scouts at the Jamboree to celebrate 21 years of scouting.

Inspecting the fences, March 1952.

The 'Prince' in Upper Parliament Street, 1952.

JAMESON, Andrew
Liverpool's 1986 Commonwealth Games Swimming gold medalist from Crosby. He won the 100 metres butterfly event in a British and Commonwealth record time of 54.07 secs, becoming the first ever British winner of that title, an event usually dominated by Australians and Canadians. 21 years old Andrew also won an individual bronze medal and previously had won a European silver medal. His sister, Helen, was also an international swimmer.

JARVIS, Frederick F.
Born 1924. Appointed General Secretary National Union of Teachers in 1975. Educated at Oldershaw Grammar School, Wallasey and Liverpool University.

JIGGER
Liverpool expression for back entry or alleyway. Expressions include "Jigger Rabbit" — a moggie (cat).

AUGUSTUS JOHN
The modern pub on Liverpool University campus named after the famed painter who lived, lectured and painted in Liverpool, and whose works can be seen in the Walker Art Gallery. One painting that isn't there, however, is the one painted by John in 1909 of Liverpool's Lord Mayor. The City Council didn't like it and it is now to be seen in Melbourne's Art Gallery in Australia.

JONES, Jack
Born in York Street, Garston, 21 March, 1913 — James Larkin Jones, working class champion and elder statesman of the union movement. This former General Secretary of the T. & G.W. Union, has fought battles on many fronts throughout a long and distinguished career. Wounded in the Spanish Civil War, this son of Liverpool has dealt with life at the sharp end. Apart from his many union appointments he also served the community as a Liverpool City Councillor. Presented the Dimbleby Lecture in 1977 and was awarded the MBE and Companion of Honour.

JONES, Ken
Liverpool born actor who has featured in many television productions, including "The Squirrels". Best remembered for his starring role in the TV play, "Going for Gold", in which he played a middle-aged marathon runner with medal aspirations. He is married to fellow Liverpool thespian, Sheila Fay.

JONES, Raymond
On Saturday, 28 October, 1961, he walked into Nems record store in Liverpool and asked for a record called "My Bonnie". When the proprietor asked him for the name of the artist, he replied "The Beatles, but you've probably never heard of them". The proprietor hadn't, but his name was Brian Epstein . . . and the rest of the story is history.

"St. Joan"

JONKER, Joan
Liverpool crusader who for more than a decade has worked tirelessly on behalf of the elderly victims of crime and violence, opening sheltered houses, holiday homes and receiving national recognition and public support.

JUMP SUNDAY
In bygone days, the Sunday prior to the running of the Grand National was a carnival day for Liverpudlians. Thousands would flock to the Course to inspect the fences, attend the fair and swop fancies for the Big Race. The cry of "I gotta horse" from the extravagantly plumed and gaily bedecked "Prince Monolulu" remains an echo of the way we were.

K

KEEGAN, Kevin
Liverpool FC soccer superstar of the Seventies. Keegan was born in Doncaster and signed for Liverpool from Scunthorpe United in 1971. In six years he won three League championship medals, an FA Cup, two UEFA cup winners medals and a European Cup winners medal.

Countless England caps and awards of every description came his way. When he arrived in Liverpool he stayed in lodgings in Lilley Grove, off Prescot Road, and before he left he resided at a luxury home with acres of grounds in North Wales. His finest game? Probably the 1977 European Cup Final in Rome when Liverpool beat Borussia Moenchengladbach 3-1. However, he didn't make the charts with his recording, "Head Over Heels in Love", in 1979.

KELLY, Margaret
(Miss Bluebell). Born in Dublin in 1910, she joined her 'adopted family' in Liverpool when a few weeks old. She started the world-famous Bluebell Girls in Paris in 1934 and from that day to this has been known as 'Miss Bluebell'.

KELLY, Margaret
A Liver Bird who could swim like a fish. Captained the British team in the 1970's and competed at European and Olympic level.

KELLY, Stan
Liverpool folk song writer. His "Liverpool Lullaby" and "I wish I was back in Liverpool" brings tears to the eyes of expatriates in Hong Kong, New York, Sydney, and Skelmersdale.

KELLY'S DIRECTORY
Originated in Liverpool (as Gore's Directory).

KENDALL, Howard
A bad back-pass by Oxford United defender Brock may have significantly changed the fortunes of the accomplished former Everton player. His managerial career at Goodison was arousing increasing impatience from the Everton faithful, and it seemed that another season was to end in failure. But that bad back pass gave Adrian Heath the opportunity to score a late Milk Cup-Tie equaliser. Everton won the replay and went on to Wembley, twice that fateful 1984 season, winning the FA Cup against Watford. The following season, Kendall became the club's first Manager of the Year as they recaptured old glories and achieved some new ones. The Championship was won, the European Cup Winners Cup won in Rotterdam and a remarkable treble foiled by a Whiteside goal in the FA Cup Final. During his playing career, Kendall was a member of the famous midfield trio (with Harvey and Ball), that masterminded Everton's 1970 championship. In his time, he was Wembley's youngest Cup Final participant when he played for Preston North End in 1964. A quiet, thoughtful manager, he represents much of what is best in professional football.

KENNY, Dr. A. J. P.
Born in Liverpool in 1931, Master of Balliol College Oxford since 1978, he was a curate in Liverpool from 1959-63, after his ordination in Rome in 1955. Author of several books on Wittgenstein, his other works include "Aristotle's Theory of the Will".

KENWRIGHT, Bill
West End producer and impressario, formerly an actor who played Gordon Clegg in "Coronation Street". One of his early stage appearances was as Shylock in the Liverpool Institute school production of "The Merchant of Venice". Also in that production was Derek Hatton, as Gratiano.

Bill returns to Liverpool every two weeks to see Everton play at Goodison.

KEYES, Clay
A former juggler with the Crazy Gang, this Liverpudlian with the transatlantic accent became a popular radio comic and compere, starring in "Danger, Men at Work" (1940) as part of the comedy duo, Haver and Lee. He created and appeared on the variety series "The Old Town Hall" with his sister, Gladys, which ran for 64 editions in its first radio series during the Second World War.

KING COTTON
Title of famous Liverpool book written by Thomas Armstrong, who was a clerk in a cotton merchant's office in the City.

KING, Hetty
Mersey Music Hall star, born in New Brighton who specialised in dressing as a man. In 1905 she introduced the perennial favourite, "All the Nice Girls Love a Sailor", to her act and another of her best known numbers was "Tell me the Old, Old Story".

She starred at the same time as many other Liverpool acts of the Music Hall Days — Billy Matchett, Beryl Orde and Harry Angers were three of the better known.

KNOTTY ASH
District of Liverpool made famous by Ken Dodd. However, tourists may search in vain for jam butty mines, diddymen, and Dicky Mint. For those still prepared to search, get a No.10 bus from Pierhead and ask the conductor to let you off at the black pudding plantation on Prescot Road.

KRAMER, Billy J
William Ashton, good-looking pop singer of Beatles era who had massive hits with "Bad to Me", (Lennon/McCartney) and "Little Children", amongst others. He is *not* the brother of Elkie Brooks.

KWOK FONG
Liverpool immigrant from China who opened a number of boarding houses to accommodate Chinese seamen and to be able to look after their welfare when they were staying in Liverpool. He opened the "Far East" restaurant in Great George Square, one of the earliest and most famous of Liverpool's multitude of Chinese restaurants. People from all over the world attended his funeral in 1969.

Clay Keyes (seated third from right) at the Empire Theatre in 1942. A
collection had been held for the RAF Benevolent Fund. His sister, Gladys, is
on his right.

Bill Kenwright taking up the challenge at Liverpool's Empire.

For Hetty King and Country.

L

LANE, CARLA

Liverpool writer who has reached hitherto unknown standards with the quality of half hour TV sitcoms, firstly with 'Butterflies' and then 'I woke up one morning' (especially the second series).

She achieved initial TV success with 'The Liver Birds' in the early 1970's (remember Ray Dunbobbin, now Ralph in Brookside, as Carol's bus driving father) and also 'Solo'. 'Butterflies' had a cult following with the humour and poignancy of its writing and playing, and 'I woke up one morning' held its audience spellbound with the quality of its script and characterisations.

LEAGUE of WELLDOERS

Started in Liverpool in 1893 by Lee Jones, the son of an Alabama cotton planter, when he was 23. A lifetime worker for the poor and underprivileged he instituted an early form of 'meals-on-wheels', delivering food to the sick in their homes. A number of local institutions have been named after him.

LEAR, Edward

The author of 'The Owl and the Pussycat', etc. Wrote his 'Book of Nonsense' whilst staying with the Earl of Derby at Knowsley Hall. The Earl was a patron and Lear wrote stories for the Earl's grandchildren. He was an influence on John Lennon ("In His Own Write", etc.) and received a mention in the Beatles hit, "Paperback Writer".

LE GALLIENNE, Richard

1866-1947. Writer and poet born in Liverpool at 55, Prescot Street. Of Channel Island descent and educated at Liverpool College. He studied accountancy for seven years in Liverpool — the City's Society of Accountants, founded in 1870, is the oldest in the country, ten years older than the Chartered Institute. His first volume of poetry was published in 1887: "My Ladies' Sonnets and Other Poems". He wrote the romantic novel 'The Quest of a Golden Girl' (1896) and was a member of the Rhymers' Club, which met at the Cheshire Cheese in Fleet Street, together with Yeats, Wilde, and co.

LENNON, John Winston/Ono

1940-1980. The Sixties, that optimistic, irreverent, magical decade had long since died when, on 9 December, 1980, we heard the news that John Lennon had been shot dead outside his apartment in New York. On that day of Lennon's death, the dream was finally over. The day has rivalled the assassination of Kennedy as a time when people recall where they were, and what they were doing when they heard the news — such was the fame of Liverpool's most famous son. At times tough, cynical, crude, hard drinking. At others, sensitive, humourous, generous, caring. The archetypal Liverpudlian and the Liverpudlian paradox.

John Lennon was born in Oxford Street Maternity Hospital on 9 October, 1940, educated at Dovedale Road School, Quarry Bank High School and Liverpool Art College. His life has been chronicled as much as anyone's this century. His departing father, the tragedy of his mother's death, Auntie Mimi, his wives — Cynthia Powell and Yoko Ono, his talent, his mistakes, his abuses.

With Paul McCartney, he was responsible for writing some of the greatest popular music and, as a member of the Beatles, at the centre of an unparalleled social phenomenon. He was an author of best selling books — "In his Own Write" and "A Spaniard in the Works" — and he continued to write memorable music after he split up with Paul McCartney. The grief felt at his death was worldwide, and the recent fifth anniversary revitalised the interest in his life and works. To many of his generation, Lennon was much more than a Beatle and a writer of extraordinary popular music. He was, more than anyone else, the man of their times.

LEWIS'S

Liverpool's best known store was founded in 1856 by David Lewis who was from a modest Jewish background. The store grew to become a huge nationwide chain, its founder, a great benefactor and showman. Later Chairman included Lord Woolton, who was also Chairman of the Conservative Party. The Liverpool store is famous for its statue by Epstein (Jacob not Brian), having been rebuilt after being blitzed during the war. The statue, erected in 1957 features in the folk song "In my Liverpool Home" ("meet under a statue exceedingly bare") and caused quite a furore when first exposed to the Liverpool public. Still, "Liverpool Resurgent" forms the centre piece of a popular Liverpool meeting or pick up point, which partly explains the Scouse saying "Yer standing there like one of Lewis's".

LEWIS, Wendy

Prolific Liverpool-born marathon walker of the early 1960's — walking from John O'Groats to Land's End. She did it in a faster time than Dr. Barbara Moore and at least 25 years before the Big Guy. For her pains, she was presented with a handbag before an Anfield match by Billy Liddell.

LIDDELL, Billy

Mersey soccer legend who signed from Scottish club Lochgelly Violett in 1938 and became Liverpool FC's most famous and celebrated player of the 1940's and 1950's. He played mostly during an era when the team struggled. So often did he appear to be carrying the team on his own broad shoulders that they were nicknamed "Liddellpool". A strong, fast forward with a terrific shot, he was a scrupulously fair player who frequently managed to score late winners or equalisers. He played many times for Scotland and, together with Stanley Matthews, was the only player to represent Great Britain in the teams of 1947 and 1955 against the Rest of Europe. Was made a JP and Bursar at Liverpool University and still lives in the City that made him a legend.

LIME STREET

Liverpool's most famous street and at times in its history, most infamous. The world-famous station was the first great railway passenger terminal built shortly after the opening of Stephenson's railway, and on which his "Rocket" ran. Opposite stands one of the world's great architectural master-pieces, St. George's Hall, built in Greek Revival style in 1854,

So this is what our boyhood idol got up to in his spare time! Billy Liddell in panto at Court Hey church as an ugly sister in 1951.

described by Queen Victoria as "worthy of Athens". And what other street anywhere, can boast two pubs as magnificent as the Crown and the Vines ("The Big House") built at the turn of the century with the style and elegance of the Edwardian age?

These two pubs, together with the Central and the Philharmonic, represent 'Cains's Folly' — the brewer who, in a spate of self indulgence, bankrupted his company building these monuments to his own ego.

The street, a traditional centre for entertainment boasting one of the province's biggest theatres, the Empire. The Theatre opened in January 1866 as The New Prince of Wales Theatre and Opera House and a name change followed in 1867 to Royal Alexandra Theatre and Opera House. It became the Empire in 1896. Until recent times The Forum, Futurist, Scala and Palais de Luxe cinema's were situated within a few yards of each other on either side of the street.

Lime Street was the legendary beat of MaggieMay, the maritime "entertainer" immortalised in the lyrics of one of Liverpool's most famous shanties.

LIPKIN, Malcolm Leyland
Composer, born in Liverpool 2 May, 1932. First came to public notice at Cheltenham Festival in 1959 with his Piano Concerto. Other works include "Sinfonia da Roma", "The

Lewis's and Liverpool . . . both resurgent.

Pursuit Symphony", and vocal piece "Four Songs of Shelley". There is a biography "The Music of Malcolm Lipkin" by H. Good.

LIVER BIRDS

Ornithologists, historians and students of Liverpudliana have long debated the mysteries, myths and mystique that surrounds the City's symbol. It would appear that the name is a corruption of 'laver bird', or Cormorant. The birds used to feed on the laver or seaweed which was available at low tide in the creeks that ran into the Mersey. What seems certain is that those birds never grew to be as tall as those that adorn the City's Liver Building — they are 18 feet in height.

Lewis's store — not after a sale but destroyed in a bombing raid in 1941.

LIVERPOOL CITY RLFC

Failed Rugby League team who played in Knotty Ash, eventually becoming Huyton RLFC with little evidence of a change in fortunes. Now operating as Runcorn Highfield.

Underprivileged youths showing a touching affection for their city's newspaper at a well-known holiday camp in 1959. Didn't the organiser do well . . . getting them to stand in the correct places!

LIVERPOOL EXPRESS

Popular hit parade group; they had top twenty hits in 1976 with "You are my Love" and "Every Man Must Have a Dream".

LIVERPOOL FC

It was John Houlding, brewer, Alderman, Justice of the Peace and Lord Mayor who, in 1892, founded Liverpool FC. IIe had originally been Everton's landlord, and had played an active role in Everton becoming an original member of the Football League. A dispute arose over the rent that Houlding was asking his fellow Evertonians, and eventually the majority moved out to newly-acquired Goodison Park. Despite losing their first match 6-0 to Rotherham, Liverpool won the Lancashire League and Liverpool Cup in their first season but, unfortunately, both trophies were stolen, and the hard-pressed board had to find the money to replace them. In 1893/94 Liverpool were admitted to the Second Division of the Football League, after the demise of Bootle FC. Liverpool won 26 of their 28 League games and after success in the Test matches (played in those days) they were promoted to Division One. A few years later they changed their strip from blue and white quarters to the familiar red. Liverpool's first championship, the first of a record 16, came in 1901 and the Club were firmly established. Among their many famous players were Sam Hardy, Elisha Scott, Bill Lacey, McKinlay, Harry Chambers, Tommy Bromilow, Hodgson, Tiny Bradshaw. The famous Kop was rebuilt in 1929, and Liverpool retained their position as one of the country's leading clubs. Despite a Championship in 1947 and a Cup Final appearance in 1950, the years in the early fifties were mostly a struggle against relegation. Eventually in 1953/54 Liverpool went down to Division 2, and their long-serving Manager, George Kay (West Ham's captain in the famous Wembley final of 1923), had been replaced by Don Welsh. Several frustrating seasons followed and then, in late 1959, the Chairman of the Club Mr. Tom (TV) Williams approached a tough charismatic Scotsman, and asked him "Would he like to manage the best club in the country?". The reply reportedly was "Why, is Matt Busby retiring?".

As a result, in December 1959, one of football's great associations began. Bill Shankly became Manager at Liverpool FC and the seeds were sown which were to culminate in the making of the world famous club of today. A first Championship for 17 years was won in 1964 and then, on 1 May, 1965, Liverpool beat Leeds United 2-1 to win the FA Cup for the first time in their history. The scenes on the team's return to Liverpool were unprecedented. An estimated 750,000 lined the streets of the City, an incredible and passionate testament to what the Club and the game meant to the people of Liverpool. Further honours followed and, by the time Shankly retired in 1974, a formula for sensible and successful management had been well established. Bob Paisley, on the Club's books since 1938, was promoted to succeed 'Shanks' and added a little more style and sophistication to the team's basic attributes. The greatest night in the Club's history followed on 25 May, 1977. Having retained the League title and unluckily lost an FA Cup Final, Liverpool beat the crack German side Borussia Moenchengladbach 3-1 to win the European Cup in Rome. It was not just the result, but the style of the performance and the marvellous contribution of the thousands of travelling fans, which provided the ideal zenith of achievement. Further European and Championship honours followed, including a hat trick of titles and four consecutive League/Milk Cups as well as individual honours to players and management. In the 1970's and 1980's Liverpool have been the dominant force in English football and many of their illustrious players have become household names; Keegan, Toshack, Souness, Dalglish, Rush, and many more. In the aftermath of Brussels, the Club faced challenging times, but their response on the pitch was inspiring as they completed a tremendous double of Championship and FA Cup victories in player-manager Dalglish's first season.

A recent convert? NO, its Liverpool's Pope-lookalike Bill Bird on his way to Rome, 1984.

Charlie Wilson the trainer, holds the Championship trophy during a street procession to celebrate the 1921/22 title win. Seated is Andy McGuigan.

Ron Yeats and Billy Stevenson hold the FA Cup aloft in Castle Street — 2 May, 1965.

A goal for Roger . . . the 'Saint' smiles . . . and Liverpool beat Ipswich 6-0 in 1964.

Smokin' Joe poolside in Rome, 1984.

LIVER HOTEL
At the junction of Crosby Road and South Road, Waterloo, a 200 year old former coaching inn saved from demolition in recent years by the considerable efforts of its patrons, who petitioned vigorously for its retention. Any visitor to the pub is likely to see the patrons still celebrating!

LIVERPOOL LOU
Sentimental folk song written by Dominic Behan, brother of Brendan.

LIVERPOOL POLICE
The first force in the country to use rubber-soled boots for nightwork. The first to use closed-circuit television in 1964 and two-way radio communication in 1934. The only force in Britain to have been on strike (1919).

The subject of a remarkable book about day-to-day police life — 'Spike Island'. And they won the English National Basketball Championships in 1970 as well as a silver medal in Tug-of-War at the 1908 Olympics. In the first round of the Olympic competition, the Liverpool team pulled the American team over the line in the first few seconds, or more appropriately in this case, "yanked" them over the line. The Americans protested that the Liverpool team's boots were illegal, with steel cleats and spikes, but the Liverpudlians maintained they were ordinary police boots. The U.S. protests were dismissed

63

64

The Liverpool Echo

THE PAPER THAT SPEAKS UP FOR MERSEYSIDE.

Since Chris Oakley was appointed editor of the Liverpool Echo the paper and its journalists have won numerous national & regional awards...

The circulation of the Echo has risen steadily under his leadership.

Here Chris Oakley shows that the Echo is much more than a leading regional paper. It is a paper that cares about the community, a paper that campaigns for a better deal for its readers, a paper that gets things done... and has fun along the way.

Who can turn people out to vote at the local government elections when apathy is normally the rule?

... the turn-out was exceptionally high at 55 per cent, probably due to a campaign by the Liverpool Echo to persuade people to vote ... THE TIMES May 1985

Well, according to the Times, we can at the Echo.

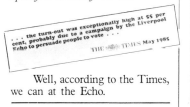

Who can turn out crowds of young people to meet Dirty Den from Eastenders?

We can. The Echo reaches readers young and old.

Who can turn out fans for Wembley, like this?

We can and when the fans go to Wembley, on what has become an annual outing from Liverpool, the Echo goes too.

Who can turn over soccer hooligans to the police?

We certainly did. These are pictures taken from videos of 13 people police wanted to interview after the Heysel stadium disaster. We were the first to print them. Our readers shopped 11 of them.

Who has the power to change the Government's mind?

The Echo. We acted as the focus for Merseyside's dismay at being left off the short list for an experimental freeport site. Our campaign reached every MP through leaflets and personal letters. We now have our freeport and the Dock and Harbour Board paid for an advertisment in the Echo to thank us for marshalling the campaign so effectively.

Who can make people reach in their pockets and come up with cash?

We can at the Echo.

Who can speak out on social issues in a way national newspapers do not dare?

We took our national award winning drugs campaign to every political party conference in the form of personal letters and leaflets to delegates. The Prime Minister gave me an interview on the strength of it and the campaign brought about the increased priority the Government is now giving to combatting drugs.

Not so well known in other parts of the country, because the national press were slow to gather the nerve to follow it up, is our campaign about the sexual abuse of children. This dealt with the incidence of sexual abuse and its aftermath so frankly that people who did not know our relationship with our readers might have expected a shoal of complaints. In fact readers sent in money to help equip a special unit to deal with child victims.

On both drugs and child abuse we set up a special hotline for readers to ring in. The drugs hotline took 2,000 calls and provided a dossier for police which led to them setting up their own hotline. The child abuse hotline took more than 400 calls and saved at least a handful of children from further suffering.

The rights:

We dealt simply with welfare entitlements. The DHSS opened an office in our foyer to deal with enquiries. The department liked the tabloid so much they asked us to print more copies to distribute all over Britain.

The wrongs:

We told Merseysiders about the Militant injustices and the stranglehold they had on Liverpool. As a result, our then Local Government Editor, Peter Phelps, was named as British Journalist of the Year, the premier award in UK journalism.

We took the words of Agnes Deacy...

...to Downing Street as part of our campaign against crime and for better compensation for its victims. The Home Secretary listened and laws are being changed along the lines we suggested.

Here at the Echo we are proud of our slogan:

THE PAPER THAT SPEAKS UP FOR MERSEYSIDE.

and they withdrew from the competition. The Liverpool team comprised: Patrick Philbin, James Clare Thomas Swindlehurst, George Smith, Daniel McLowry, William Greggan, Thomas Butler, and Alexander Kidd.

LIVERPOOL RUFC

The oldest public or 'open' Rugby club in the world, founded in 1857, played at St. Michael's, Aigburth, until the end of the 1985/86 season when they relocated to St. Helens. The club provided three England players (Lyon, Tobin and Clayton) for the very first international match, played in Edinburgh on 27 March, 1871. Kewley of Liverpool was the England captain in their first international with 15 players (previously 20-a-side) against Ireland on 5 February, 1877, at the Oval. The club achieved a remarkable and unique distinction just prior to the First World War when the captains of England (Poulton), Ireland (Lloyd), and Scotland (Turner), were all on their books. R. W. Poulton was a brilliant three-quarter, the idol of English rugby in his day. He once scored 4 tries in a match against France in Paris and 5 tries for Oxford in a Varsity match. The try he scored against South Africa's tourists in 1912 was the first ever scored against them by a home counties' international player, and one of the most memorable ever. In all he played 17 times for England, several as an inspiring skipper, in a career cut tragically short. He was killed in the First World War.

In recent years, Higgins, Regan, Beese, Roughley and Simms all represented their country. The club's most distinguished recent player was locally-born Mike Slemen, England's most-capped winger of all time — now a teacher at Merchant Taylor's, Crosby.

Slemen played in the international against Australia in 1981 when the impressively-endowed Erica Roe appeared on the pitch at half-time, topless. It appears that captain Billy Beaumont's pep talk was interrupted by the comment, "Billy there's a woman on the field with your bum on her chest".

Liverpool St. Helens line up for their first match.

The first match after the merger with St. Helens was played on 31 August, 1986 and the newly named Liverpool St. Helens beat Aberavon 10-3. The team on that historic occasion was: Askew, Tanner, Simms, Wellans, Appleton, Jeffrey, Jones, Robbins, Rabbitt (Capt), Chubb, Hale, McKeown, Morris, Hescott and Catlow.

LIVERPOOL PENNANTS

The name, given to the rope yarns used on a sailor's coat instead of buttons. The usage can be extended to describe the beckets and toggles which fasten duffel coats.

LIVERPOOLS

Greetings to the citizens of the townships of Liverpool New South Wales, Australia, Liverpool New York State, USA, Liverpool Nova Scotia, Canada.

It is flattering that your towns are named after the great city on the Mersey. We hope that you will visit us soon.

LORD MAYOR

Liverpool no longer has one. But the first Mayor was William Fitzadam in 1351 and the last, Councillor Stanley Airey.

LORD NELSON LIVES IN LIVERPOOL 8

Title of play written by Philip Martin, performed at London's Royal Court in 1974.

LOTTERY

Appropriately named first winner of Aintree Grand National in 1839, ridden by J. Mason.

LOWE, John

Liverpool-born jockey who rode K-Battery to victory in the 1986 Lincoln Handicap at 25-1.

LOWRY, Malcolm

A legend in America. This son of Merseyside, whose father was a sea captain and cotton merchant, wrote 'Under the Volcano' in which he drew on his own personal struggle with drink. Other works include 'Hear us, O Lord, from Heaven Thy dwelling Place'. He died in 1957, aged 48.

LUCY, Sir Henry

1843-1924. Born at Crosby, Liverpool, he wrote for many years as "Toby MP" for Punch.

Editor of the parliamentary staff of the Daily News, he had close personal relationships with many leading politicians of his day.

LYCEUM CLUB

The second oldest of Liverpool's gentlemen's clubs, founded as a newsroom and library in 1803, originally in Bold Street. Its members are 'proprietors' and they, and the members of the City's other remaining gentlemen's clubs, were the subject of a BBC Radio 4 programme in January 1986.

The club is now situated in Paradise Street and the original building has been bought by the Post Office to be opened in 1987 as the Northern Branch of the National Postal Museum.

LYON, John

Merseyside boxer who equalled the record number of ABA titles when he became flyweight champion in 1986, his fifth title (Dick McTaggart, Terry Waller, and Merseyside's George Gilbody also won 5). An Olympic and 1986 Commonwealth Games representative.

A visitor from the East tries the tigers tooth for luck at the old NatWest Bank building in Water Street.

The Steble Fountain in William Brown Street provides a splash for these Liverpool children on a hot summer day.

M

MACE, Jem
Middleweight boxer whose career spanned 36 years; the longest recorded anywhere in the world. He died in 1910, aged 79, and is buried in Anfield cemetery.

MAGHULL
Dormitory town of Liverpool on A59, original home of the Grand National which was held there in 1837. The first race was won by "The Duke" ridden by a Mr. Potts. There were 4 starters.
The home for epileptics, opened 1888, is the oldest in Britain and the second oldest in the world.

MAKEPEACE, Harry
One of Everton FC's double internationals, he played for England at cricket (4 tests — 1920/21) scoring 117 in one match, and at football as a right-half. Played in 487 matches for Lancashire and became Chief Coach at Old Trafford on his retirement from playing. At soccer, he won an FA Cup medal with Everton in 1906 and played ten times for England between 1906-1912. He died in 1952.
The famous Makepeace bat, autographed by many of the great players of the 1930's, is displayed in the reception area of the Liverpool Echo offices in Old Hall Street.

MALAM, Colin
The Sunday Telegraph's leading football writer who always ensures his local bias never intrudes on his impartiality.

MANCHESTER
Thirty miles from Liverpool and always will be.

MARATHON MIRTHQUAKE
At the Royal Court Theatre in Liverpool in 1974 Ken Dodd made the Guinness Book of Records when he told jokes for 3 hours 6 minutes 30 seconds non-stop. It is not known how many tickling sticks he went through.

MARSDEN, Gerry
Born at 8 Menzies Street, Liverpool 8, he rocketed to fame in the early 1960's at the time of the Mersey Beat boom . . . unique at the time in that his first three records with the Pacemakers all made No.1 in the pop charts. Wrote "Ferry 'cross the Mersey" for the film of the same name, his recording of "You'll Never Walk Alone" was adopted by the Kop supporters at Anfield as a football anthem, and copied at grounds all over the country. Appeared with Dame Anna Neagle in "Charlie Girl" on the London stage and in 1985 re-recorded "You'll Never Walk Alone" to return to the top of the charts as a fund-raiser for the Bradford City soccer fire victims.

MARY ELLENS
The name given to a rare breed of Liverpudlian. These characteristic old women finally disappeared from the city streets in the late fifties. Clad in long dresses and petticoats with black lace shawls, they could often be seen around Scotland Road carrying the washing back from the wash-house balanced on their heads. In earlier days, however, the name was used for Liverpudlian prostitutes.

Shawls but no washing — Liverpool, 1929.

MASEFIELD, John

1878-1967. Poet Laureate from 1930 and honoured with the Order of Merit. He spent three years (1891-1894) on the training ship 'Conway' on the Mersey.

This experience obviously influenced his later work as the Herefordshire-born writer produced much of his poetry and novels about the sea. "Sea Fever" ('I must go down to the sea again, to the lonely sea and the sky') and "Cargoes" being the most famous. His Liverpool poems are "The Wanderer" and "Liverpool 1890".

MASTERMIND

Liverpool had two representatives in the 1986 Final of the prestigious BBC quiz: Philip McDonald, a school teacher at St. Francis Xavier's School and Michael Formby, a chartered surveyor from Aintree.

MATCH OF THE DAY

The first telecast for the long running BBC soccer programme was from Anfield in August 1964. Liverpool beat Arsenal 3-2. The commentator was Kenneth Wolstenholme. Liverpool featured on the first all-colour programme five years later, in 1969.

MAYBRICK

The name at the centre of one of Liverpool's most famous murder trials. Florence Maybrick, an American, was accused of murdering her husband, James, a wealthy Liverpool merchant at their home — Battlecrease House, Riversdale Road, Aigburth. It was alleged Florence removed the arsenic from flypaper to poison her husband, who, at 50, was 24 years older than his wife. Florence admitted adultery, but protested her innocence to the crime of murder.

PRICE SIXPENCE.

Mrs. MAYBRICK'S OWN STORY
"My Fifteen Lost Years"

C. ARTHUR PEARSON, LIMITED.

Amidst much controversy she was sentenced to death by Mr. Justice Stephens and a Liverpool jury in 1889. There was much public protest and a plea by the American Consul. Mrs. Maybrick was reprieved and was returned to America where she obtained release in 1904. She died penniless, aged 80. She had returned just once to Liverpool, to see a Grand National.

MAYER, Joseph

Liverpool businessman and great benefactor. He donated his world-famous collection of mediaeval ivories to Liverpool Museum and amongst his collection of Anglo-Saxon relics on display is the famous Kingston Brooch. He was the benefactor of Bebington's first public library and the first person in Europe to successfully grow the Victoria Regina, the giant Amazon water lily, in the open air. He died in 1886.

McBAIN, Neil

The former Everton, Liverpool and Scottish international, became the oldest Football League player to play in a league match when he played in goal, an emergency measure, for New Brighton against Hartlepool on 15 March, 1947 (a Division 3 North match). He was 51 years 4 months old. At the time he was New Brighton's Manager. They left the League at the end of the 1950/51 season having joined the Third Division North in 1923/24 and had their best season in 1924/25 when they finished third.

McCABE, John

Composer/musician born in Huyton, Liverpool in 1939 and educated at Liverpool Institute. He has composed for violin, piano and organ and his recordings include a 16-record set of the complete piano music of Haydn. He received a special award in 1975 from the Composers Guild of Great Britain for services to British music and the Ivor Novello Award in 1977 for his theme tune for TV's "Sam".

Other compositions include the orchestral "The Chagall Windows" and he has written reviews for the "Guardian" and "New Statesman". He was appointed Director, London College of Music, in 1983.

McCARTNEY, Paul

The world's most famous and successful pop star was born at Walton Hospital, Liverpool on 18 June, 1942, the first son of Mary Patricia (née Mohin) and James McCartney, themselves both of Liverpool.

Paul's father was himself a part-time musician, playing piano in Jim Mac's Jazz Band, appearing at local dances in the Liverpool area.

Paul was educated at Stockton Wood Road School (at the time the largest infant school in the country), Joseph Williams Primary School, Belle Vale, and Liverpool Institute High School. On 15 June, 1956, at a church fête at St. Peter's, Woolton, Paul met John Lennon and soon afterwards joined John's group, the Quarrymen.

A left-handed guitarist of some merit and a songwriter extraordinaire, McCartney survived the heady days of Beatlemania and has retained his position at the top of the world's music industry. Firstly, through forming the group, Wings, and in recent years largely as a solo artist or in association with other giants of the pop world such as Stevie Wonder and Michael Jackson.

After a much publicised relationship with actress Jane Asher, he eventually married Linda Eastman on 12 March, 1969, at Marylebone Registry office, and they live now in Sussex with their children.

Although most Beatles' songs were credited to Lennon-McCartney many of their compositions were individually penned with the other adding his own ideas to complete the finished product. McCartney's influence tended to be sweeter, more sentimental than Lennon's but the combination of both their talents resulted in the magnificent musical legacy that we are left with.

In recent years, Paul has explored other fields, notably the film "Give My Regards to Broad Street", but what seems certain is that he has much to offer the future musical and entertainment world.

McGANN, Paul

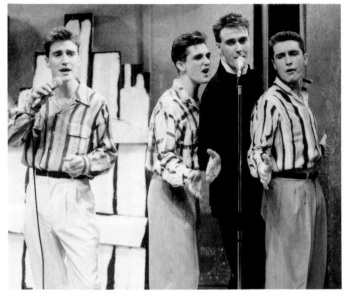

Emerging from the family pop group, he had a big break as the Scouse snooker player in BBC TV's 'Give us a Break', but his performance as Percy Topliss in Alan Bleasdale's 'The Monocled Mutineer' was worthy of a 147 and put him in line for a major TV award.

Brother Mark played John in the hit musical 'Lennon' and also played him on American TV in 'Love Story'.

Younger brother Steve featured in the BBC TV sitcom, 'Help', playing Tex in Joe Boyle's comedy series about three unemployed Scouse likely lads.

Singer, songwriter, actor Joe, the eldest of the McGann brothers completes this talented quartet.

McGEAR, Mike

Member of "Scaffold" and author of "Thank-U-Very-Much" a fond reminiscence of being Paul McCartney's younger brother, which he still is.

McGOUGH, Roger

The Liverpool poet. The timbre of his voice and his distinctive delivery seems to add a dimension to the readings of his funny, sad, ironic poetry of our times.

Born in Liverpool in 1937, the son of a docker, he was educated at St. Mary's College. He had a very successful career with the group, Scaffold, in the 1960's and enjoyed massive chart hits "Thank-U-Very-Much", and "Lily The Pink". His considerable output of poetry has been published in many anthologies including Watchwords, After The Merrymaking, Gig, Waiving At Trains and Sky in the Pie.

His collaboration with Adrian Henri and Brian Patten was responsible for helping to popularise poetry in the late 60's. A supporter of Everton FC.

McGOVERN, Pete

Songwriter best known for "In My Liverpool Home".

McKENNA, John

Ulster immigrant largely responsible for Liverpool FC achieving Football League status. Shortly after becoming a Liverpool FC Committee member, he signed 13 Scottish professionals and Liverpool became known affectionately as MacLiverpool. "Honest" John was Chairman at Liverpool between 1909-1914 and 1917-1919 and, for 25 years, President of the Football League.

McLOUGHLIN, Joey

The Liverpudlian who, by getting 'on his bike', became the first Briton since 1976 to win the gruelling Round-Britain Milk Race in June 1986. His margin of victory was the biggest for 20 years and his winning time, 40 hours 38 minutes 20 seconds. The previous British winner was another Merseysider, Bill Nickson.

Previously, McLoughlin had been the youngest rider to compete in the World Amateur Road Race Championships

and he was the winner, at 20, of the 1985 Sealink International.

MECCANO

Manufactured at the company's Edge Lane works, they delighted generations of technically minded youngsters in pre-Lego days. The early sets are now collectors' items.

Meccano was invented by Frank Hornby who was born in Liverpool in 1863. The patent for Meccano sets was granted in 1901 and in the early days he and his assistant carried the boxed sets to the first shop prepared to sell them, Philip Son and Nephew.

In 1903 Hornby bought the plant in Binns Road and shortly afterwards began making Hornby Trains and Dinky Toys. The invention which had started in the workshop of his home making toy cranes for his sons, was to make him a millionaire and his company eventually had branches in New York, Paris, Berlin and in other cities around the world.

He was MP for Everton between 1931-1935 and he died in 1937.

MELIA, Jimmy

Liverpool and England soccer star. As manager, took Brighton to their first-ever Cup Final in 1983. Member of famous Liverpool bookmaker family.

MELLY, Andre

Represented the dramatic branch of the Melly family with many prominent stage and TV roles in the 50's/60's. Brother George and Andre are related to Florence, notable Liverpool benefactor of schools, etc.

MELLY, George

Goodtime George; writer, jazz singer, art critic, raconteur, as surrealist as the paintings he admires. With John Chilton's Footwarmers delights his large cult following with renditions of bawdy blues ballads in a style that is exclusively his. His books, amongst them the autobiographical "Rum Bum and Concertina", and "Scouse Mouse" extended the legend. Received the Critic of the Year Award 1970. Also wrote "Flook" cartoon strips and film scripts.

MELVILLE, Herman

American writer most famous for 'Moby Dick', he made several visits to Liverpool and wrote a lengthy description of Liverpool's waterfront and shipping in 'Redburn'.

25, MENLOVE GARDENS EAST

The "address" that featured in one of Liverpool's most famous murder mysteries. William Herbert Wallace was a 52-year old Prudential Insurance agent in Liverpool at the beginning of 1931. On 19 January, a telephone message was left at Wallace's chess club in Liverpool, for Wallace to call the following evening at the home of R. M. Qualtrough, 25 Menlove Gardens East, for a business appointment.

The following evening Wallace left his home at 29, Wolverton Street, shortly after 6 o'clock to keep his appointment with Mr. Qualtrough. He caught the tram to Smithdown Road and headed off to where he imagined his destination to be. But despite much searching and enquiry, Wallace did not find the address or keep his appointment with Mr. Qualtrough. He eventually returned home shortly before 9 p.m. and, unable to gain access he called on the assistance of his neighbours, Mr. & Mrs. Johnston, and eventually gained entry. Once inside they found the body of Wallace's wife, Julia, a frail music-loving 50-year old, who had been savagely beaten to death. She was wearing a charred mackintosh as well as her normal clothing. A little while afterwards Wallace was arrested and accused of the crime.

At his trial, Wallace's neighbours, the Johnstons, gave evidence and commented on how calmly Wallace had behaved when they discovered his wife's body. Several witnesses were called who stated that they'd seen and spoken to Wallace on that January evening of his search for Menlove Gardens East. But it was also established that the phone call to the chess club had been made from a telephone box near to Wolverton Street (Anfield 1672). Despite Wallace's insistence on his innocence, he was sentenced to death at St. George's Hall on 25 April, 1931.

An appeal followed and as a consequence the sentence was quashed. Wallace retired to the country and made extensive security arrangements at his house, convinced that his wife's killer would try to murder him as well. Wallace maintained that he knew the killer and subsequent theories included that the murderer of Julia Wallace was a business associate of her husband's and that the motive was robbery.

Wallace died of cancer on 26 February, 1933. In today's Liverpool, as was the case in 1931, you can find Menlove Gardens North, Menlove Gardens South and Menlove Gardens West, but like William Herbert Wallace on that fateful evening of 20 January, you will search in vain for Menlove Gardens East. As for the true identity of R. M. Qualtrough and who made the call from Anfield 1672 . . . the mystery remains unsolved.

JOE MERCER

Genial and talented Mersey football man who captained Arsenal in the 1950 Cup Final against Liverpool, and who broke his leg, which ended his playing career, in a match at Highbury against Liverpool a few years later.

Joe, a lifelong Evertonian and former player, was a successful manager, including, for a time, caretaker-manager of England, and a wise sage on the game. However, he did provide a lovely gaffe on a television football panel some years ago when describing the great Dutch player Cruyf, as Johann Sebastian. Obviously he had another half Bach on his mind!

MERSEY RAILWAY
The World's first underwater railway, 750 trains a day used to travel under the Mersey between Central Station, James Street and Hamilton Square in the early 1900's — a train every three minutes each way. The first railway to be converted from steam to electricity (1903), it was a tremendous engineering feat when completed. The modern Merseyrail is one of the best systems in the country.

MERSEYSIPPI Jazz Band
Talented group of musicians who deserved to do well if only for the originality of their name.

MILLS, Alan
Wimbledon's championship referee comes from Formby and was educated at Waterloo Grammar School. A former British Davis Cup player, who was ranked 4th in Britain, he once beat Rod Laver in a tournament in the year the great Australian champion won one of his Wimbledon titles.

MISCELLANY
● The first gorilla to be seen in Britain was at Liverpool Docks in 1876.
● At one time, two double English soccer and cricket internationals — Sharp and Makepeace — lived in the same Dingle street, Rosslyn Street. The young Arthur Askey was also resident there at that time.
● On the day of John Lennon's funeral in December 1980, some U.S. radio stations stayed silent for ten minutes.
● "Tipperary Tim" was the only horse to finish in the 1929 Grand National.
● A sign in Ma Boyle's Oyster Bar in Old Hall Street said, "Gentlemen are requested not to smoke before 2.00 p.m." . . . the smoke impaired the flavour of the oysters.
● Ted Sagar, the famous Everton goalkeeper, was on their books as a player, from 26 March, 1929, until May 1953 — a record. He became licensee of the Blue Anchor on retiring from the game.
● The well known historian, A. J. P. Taylor, was born at 29 Barrett Road, Birkdale, in 1906.
● The Liverpool School of Tropical Medicine, the world's first (founded 1898), appointed Sir Ronald Ross as its first lecturer. Ross went on to win a Nobel Prize for tracing the disease malaria to the mosquito.
● The Mersey football teams have had many players who have been "disguised" by their nicknames: The Flying Pig, Barney Rubble, The Iron Lung, Crazy Horse, Eggo, Mae West, Nivvy, Golden Vision, Rowdy, Black Harry, Rambo, Super Sub, Big and Little Bamber, Douglas Bader. Can you name them?
● Paul McCartney's record, "Mull of Kintyre", was the first record in Britain registering sales of over 2 million.
● Southport's Jimmy Rimmer played 8 minutes for two European Cup winners' medals, substitute for Stepney (Man. Utd., 1968) replaced by Spink after injury (Aston Villa, 1982).
● 105,000 watched the FA Cup derby game in March 1967. 65,000 at Goodison and 40,000 at Anfield on closed circuit television. Everton won 1-0 (Ball).
● A Liverpool Echo reader's suggestion for the underground Lime Street pedestrian way was: Sub Lime Way.

72

● The first 'modern' package tour was introduced by Thomas Cook in 1845. The destination? Liverpool and North Wales.
● The Wavertree 'mystery', called that because of an anonymous donor. Later found to be a member of the Holt shipping family. Still called "The Mizzie".
● George Formby (Jnr.), the famous ukelele star, was born blind. As a small child his mother took him on a ferry across the Mersey. During the trip he had a coughing fit and it suddenly became apparent that he could see.
● The first Irish Nationalist to sit for an English constituency was T. P. O'Connor, Bootle, from 1880.
● On the night that the Beatles first appeared on U.S. TV's 'Ed Sullivan Show' 9 February, 1964, reported crimes in the USA were the lowest for 50 years. An estimated 73 million watched the show, a record at the time.
In March 1964, the Beatles had the top 5 records in the Billboard Hot 100 Singles Chart. Can't Buy Me Love, Twist and Shout, She Loves You, I Want to Hold Your Hand, and Please Please Me.
● An estimated 70,000 people watched the country's first balloon ascent by J. Sadler on Merseyside in 1812.
● In season 1927/28 'Dixie' Dean needed 9 goals in 3 matches to beat George Camsell's League record. He hit 2, 4 and 3 in those matches to beat the record with 60 goals.
● The Princes Road Synagogue was the largest in Britain when built in 1874, accommodating 900 people.
● Pilkington's produced the biggest plate glass window ever in 1951 for the Festival of Britain, 50' x 8'.

Wash-and-brush-up for the Duke of Wellington in 1971.

● Frank Atkinson, architect and designer of ships interiors, was responsible for the new Adelphi Hotel completed in 1912. He was also responsible for Selfridges store in Oxford Street, London.
● Distinguished former pupils of Liverpool College not mentioned elsewhere include Baron Stopford of Fallowfield — the anatomist who was first Chairman, Manchester Regional Hospital Board and a Freeman of that City; Sir Richard Glazebrook — the first Director of the National Physical Laboratory and Andrew Forsyth the famous Cambridge University mathematician.
● George Holt, member of the famous Liverpool family, founded in 1844 Britain's first girls' day grammar school at Blackburne House.

MOLONEY, Peter
Schoolteacher who became spokesman and commentator on the Scouse dialect and other features of Scouse life in the 1960's and 70's. He is still "racontouring" the after-dinner circuit.

MONUMENTS AND MEMORIALS
There are many notable monuments, plaques and memorials on Merseyside honouring a variety of distinguished people and events. Certainly the biggest is the Wellington monument at the head of William Brown Street: 150 feet in height, designed by George Lawson and inaugurated in 1863. The Duke's features are cast in bronze from cannon taken from

Service of dedication, the Merchant Navy Memorial, 1952.

Waterloo. Across the way, memorials in the St. George's Hall area include those to Sir Arthur Forwood, Liverpool Mayor in 1877 and Secretary to the Admiralty; William Rathbone (the sixth William), MP and a founder of Liverpool University and District Nursing; Gladstone, Monsignor Nugent and Canon Major Lester. A monument in St. John's Gardens is to Alexander Balfour, shipowner, merchant, Liverpool benefactor and tea totaller. He objected to Walker, the brewer, gifting the Walker Art Gallery to the City on the grounds of Walker's occupation.

In other parts of the City there are memorials to Queen Victoria, George III, Edward VII, George V and Queen Mary, Prince Albert, Disraeli and — at the Walker Art Gallery, which was designed by local man Cornelius Sherlock — Michelangelo and Raphael. At the south-east corner of St. George's Hall is a statue to Major-General William Earle (1833-1885), a distinguished Liverpool native who commanded the relief forces to General Gordon and was killed leading an attack at the Battle of Kirkeban in the Sudan.

Again in the St. George's Hall area is the impressive monument to the King's Liverpool Regiment and the men lost in wars in South Africa, Afghanistan and Burma. There is an unusual plaque in St. John's Gardens to the French prisoners who died in Liverpool during the Napoleonic wars.

At the Pierhead, the podium was erected by the Liverpool Trades Council to celebrate its 125th anniversary with a plaque by Arthur Dooley depicting the 'Unity of European Labour'. An award winner, it was commissioned to celebrate Britain's entry into the Common Market. Also at the Pierhead is a memorial to Sir Alfred Lewis Jones. Jones developed trade between Liverpool and West Africa and the West Indies as a partner with the Elder Dempster Line, and was largely responsible for popularising the banana in this country. He was the founder of the Liverpool School of Tropical Medicine. Towards St. Nicholas' Church is the Engineers' memorial dedicated to "all the heroes of the Titanic's engine-room who were lost at sea".

At the Town Hall is a bust of George Canning, Liverpool MP and briefly Prime Minister, the last to die in office in 1827, and at the entrance to the Mersey Tunnel, a memorial to Sir Archibald Salvidge, Lord Mayor and Chairman of the First Tunnel committee. Around Liverpool there are also to be found memorials to Nelson, Columbus, William Huskisson MP — the railway's first passenger fatality — the Merchant Navy and the American Coat of Arms are carved in stone at Compton House, Marks and Spencer's store in Church Street. In Birkenhead's Hamilton Square is a statue of John Laird, founder of modern Birkenhead, and at Birkenhead Park — an obelisk commemorates John Somerville Jackson, the originator of the Park. Opened in 1847, on the same day as the town's first major dock, it is one of the country's finest public parks and a prototype of New York's famous Central Park.

MONSARRAT, Nicholas
The author of "The Cruel Sea" was born the son of a distinguished surgeon, in Rodney Street, Liverpool, in 1910. His most famous novel was published in 1951 and was later made into a film starring Jack Hawkins. His other famous novels include "The Tribe that Lost Its Head", "The Story of Esther Costello", "The White Rajah", and "The Nylon Pirates". He spent his last years living in Malta and was buried at sea, as was his wish.

MOORE, Ray
Popular radio and TV presenter who gets up in the middle of the night in order to entertain fellow insomniacs, or is it because Big Alma kicks him out?
Draws upon his Liverpool background and uses Scouse mythology to combat Wogan's blarney.

MOORES, Sir John
Entrepreneur who found Liverpool to be a location conducive to his commercial creativity. Founded the Littlewoods organisation, through innovative marketing. His football pools delivered hope on a weekly basis to millions of homes. He followed this by pioneering 'mail order' and now delivers more tangible items to more homes than any other company in Britain. The John Moores Modern Art Exhibition at Liverpool's Walker Art Gallery is the country's premier event of its kind. Former Chairman of Everton Football Club where his influence was prominent in the 1960's, when Everton FC where known as the Mersey Millionaires. Celebrated his 90th birthday in January 1986.

MORGAN, John
Liverpool golfer who, at 42 and after 18 years on the professional circuit, won his first European title in June 1986, the Jersey 'Open' at La Moye. He won at the first extra hole of a 'sudden death' play-off beating Australia's Peter Fowler.

MORRIS, Rev. Marcus
Creator of "Eagle" comic, a glossy innovative boys' weekly when it first appeared on 14 April, 1950. Dan Dare (created by Southport's Frank Hampson) adorned its colourful first page and the comic achieved tremendous popularity in the 1950's. Printed by the Aintree firm of Eric Bemrose, a sister comic "Girl" eventually followed along with "Swift" and "Robin". Marcus Morris was vicar at St. James Church, Birkdale, between 1945-50.

MORRIS, Robert
The Liverpudlian who signed the American Declaration of Independence in 1776. His story was both one of America's most spectacular early success stories and one of its most tragic failures.
Born in Liverpool in 1734, his father was a tobacco agent. Morris eventually settled in America and became a successful financier and merchant. After helping in the making of the American Constitution he became a Senator for Pennsylvania and, when the economy was in difficulty, accepted the post of Superintendent of Finance. He stabilised the economy and issued "Morris Notes" — his signature guaranteeing personal credit — before founding the Bank of North America, America's first national bank.
After speculating in land deals in the West he became bankrupt in 1798 and spent three years in a debtors' prison. He died in Philadelphia on 8 May, 1806.

MOSS, Rev. Reginald Heber
County cricketer with perhaps the oddest career of all. Born at Huyton, Liverpool 1868, he was an Oxford Blue, 1889, and played for Liverpool and District against the Australians in 1893. He then went 32 years before playing his one county game for Worcestershire v. Gloucestershire in May 1925, when he was 57 years of age. He died in 1956.

MUSIC FESTIVAL
The North-West's biggest Music Festival held at the Festival Gardens in June 1986, incorporated rock, country, jazz and variety. Sponsored by Ty-phoo the acts included China Crisis, Gerry and The Pacemakers, Searchers, Hillsiders, Phil Brady and The Ranchers, Liverpool Ceilidh Band, and the award-winning Liverpool Ladies' Barbershop Singers and Male Barbershop Harmony Club.

Monsarrat in Liverpool, 1955.

N

NAVAL VISITS

HMS Liverpool, a Type 42 destroyer built in Birkenhead, has paid many happy visits to the Mersey.

N.A.L.G.O.
Founded by a 26-year old clerk, Herbert Blain, in the Liverpool Town Clerks' Department as the Liverpool Municipal Officers' Guild. Blain eventually moved to London to set up the National Union in 1905.

NATWEST BANK
The Bank chose Princes Road, Liverpool, for the location of Britain's first drive-in bank.

NEWMAN, Ernest
1868-1959. Real name William Roberts. Music critic of the Sunday Times, 1920-1958, and author of works on Strauss, Elgar, Liszt, and The Life of Richard Wagner (4 volumes). Started his career as a clerk in the Bank of Liverpool after education at Liverpool College and Liverpool University, where he later lectured. Also wrote for Manchester Guardian, Birmingham Daily Post and the Observer.

NEWNES, Billy
Liverpool-born jockey who won a Classic — The Oaks — on Time Charter in 1982, whilst still an apprentice. Was banned for three years by the Jockey Club in 1984 for accepting an illegal payment.
His disqualification was reduced from three years to two-and-a-half by the Jockey Club in February 1986.

NEWTON, John
1725-1807. Slave-ship Captain who worked for the Liverpool slave ship owner, Manesty, and who wrote "Amazing Grace". He went to sea as a boy and eventually became involved in the infamous slave trade. His increasing doubts about the morality of his occupation resulted in the publication of "An Authentic Narrative" in 1764. He became a Tide Surveyor whilst waiting to enter the church, and then left his home in Edmund Street, Liverpool, to take up his new position as Curate at Olney in Buckinghamshire. There he became a strong influence on William Cowper, who lived with Newton and his wife and helped Newton with Olney Hymns, whilst Cowper himself was recovering from a breakdown.
Among Newton's most famous hymns are "Glorious Things of Thee Are Spoken" and "How Sweet the Name of Jesus Sounds". His most famous work has become one of the most popular of modern anthems and, amazingly, a Hit Parade success. Judy Collins' recording reached No.5 in Britain and was a world-wide hit in 1970 and in subsequent years. The Pipes and Drums and Military Band of the Royal Scots' Dragoon Guards were No.1 for 5 weeks in 1972. The Kop at Anfield even adopted the tune as a tribute to Bill Shankly. Newton was a leading figure in the Evangelical revival in the Church of England, and he influenced many in the English-speaking world with his revival of Calvinistic views.
He wrote his own epitaph.

Here lies John Newton, Clerk. Once an infidel and libertine, a servant of slaves in Africa was, by the rich mercy of our Lord and Saviour Jesus Christ, preserved, restored, pardoned and appointed to preach the faith he had long laboured to destroy.

NIMMO, Derek

Cultured Liverpool-born actor (19.9.1933) who once did a roller-skating act with his wife. His many film, TV and stage roles have included "The Amorous Prawn", "Charlie Girl", "The World of Wooster" and on TV, "Oh Brother", "All Gas and Gaiters" and "Hell's Bells" in 1986.
His polished playing of rather pompous 'assistant managers' suggests he may have spent a lot of his formative days in Hendersons, Bon Marché or George Henry Lee's.

NOBLETT, Ma
The "toffee woman" who traditionally scatters sweetmeats to the Everton faithful before matches.

NOOK, The
Liverpool's famous Chinese pub in Nelson Street. For many years the drinkers dreaded "Last orders, please!" has been said in Chinese.
Former proprietor, Mrs. Eileen Jones — famed for her range of exotic hats — introduced the tradition which lasts to this day. Within walking distance of the pub is a wide selection of Chinese restaurants and the pagoda-styled Community and Cultural Centre of a Hundred Harmonies.

NUGENT, Father
Liverpool-born Catholic priest who provided food, shelter and education for thousands of Liverpool urchins in the 19th century. He established an Institute for boys, opened day schools, a home for destitute women and was the first Catholic chaplain at Walton gaol. He was also instrumental in changing legislation, making Liverpool the first place in the country to outlaw street-trading by children. Also a founder of the Catholic Times. This great benefactor, later to become Monsignor, had a nine-column obituary in the Daily Post on his death. A statue to his memory stands in St. John's Gardens. His Protestant friend and helper, Canon Major Lester of St. Mary's, Kirkdale, is also remembered by a monument in the Gardens.

O

OBSERVATORY

At Bidston, where the world's tides are predicted. Built in 1866, an important centre for the study of scientific research into tidal movements, preparation of tide tables and seismological observations.

Originally built by the Mersey Docks and Harbour Board, the Institute of Oceanographic Services is the world's leading tidal authority. It was here that the vital information and data was produced prior to the D-Day landings.

Although still called Bidston observatory the last telescope was removed and sent to Liverpool Museum in 1969.

ONE O'CLOCK GUN

Previous generations of Merseysiders were ensured that their afternoons got off to a bang with the daily time check. The gun was first fired on 21 September, 1867, and eventually situated at Morpeth Dock, Birkenhead being triggered electronically from Bidston Observatory. The custom ended on 18 July, 1969.

OSMOND, Little Jimmy

American junior member of family group, took a short cut to success in 1972 with "Long Haired Lover from Liverpool", which reached No.1 in the Hit Parade.

O'SULLIVAN, Paula

Paula St. John Lawrence Lawler Byrne Strong Stevenson Callaghan Hunt Milne Smith Thompson Shankly Bennett Paisley O'Sullivan was the daughter born to Peter O'Sullivan in April 1966, and christened thus. It is considered highly unlikely that Mr. O'Sullivan was an Evertonian.

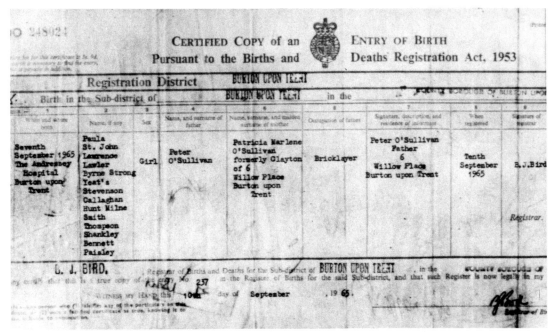

Peter O'Sullivan, originally from Fazakerley, Liverpool, and proof of Paula.

O'CONNOR, Tom

Former Liverpool schoolteacher who, after enjoying great success in local clubs with his 'slices of scouse life', became nationally-known as comic and compére of "London Night Out".

Continually asking people to "Name That Tune", he has since developed into a smooth and all-round TV entertainer.

OLIVER, Stephen

Born Liverpool, 1950 — musician and composer. His operas include "Duchess of Malfi", "A Fur Coat for Summer", "Tom Jones", "The Girl and The Unicorn" and "Beauty and the Beast". He also wrote for the musical, "Blondel", and "Nicholas Nickleby", suite for brass quintet. His choral music includes: "A String of Beads" Cantata (1980), and "Seven Words" Cantata (1985).

OULTON, Brian

Began in rep. at Liverpool Playhouse, the Liverpool-born veteran has appeared in "Carry On" films, "Hancock's Half Hour", "I'm all right, Jack", "Thirty Nine Steps", "Brideshead Revisited", "The Old Curiosity Shop", etc.

OUR KID

Teenybopper Liverpool group who had a huge hit with "You just might see me cry" in 1976. It reached No.2 in the charts, and they were never heard of or seen again. Also an endearing Scouse term for younger member of the family.

OWEN, Alun

Liverpool-Welsh playwright best known for "Progress to the Park", "No Trams to Lime Street", and the screenplay of the Beatles' first film "Hard Days' Night".

OWEN OWEN

Son of a Welsh farmer, he opened his first shop in Liverpool in 1868, at 121 London Road. Today the organisation has departmental stores all over Britain and abroad.

P

PADDY'S MARKET
Liverpool's most famous market, established in 1826 and originally sited in Scotland Road, still exists today, though it can now be found in Great Homer Street. St. Martins Market attracted many of the sailors who docked in Liverpool during its hey-day, and their multi-national presence helped to make its colour, character and atmosphere.

PAISLEY, Bob
The most successful manager in British football was born in Hetton le Hole and, after playing for Bishop Auckland, arrived in Liverpool in 1938. A tough tackling wing-half, he survived being left out of the 1950 Cup Final team, after scoring in the semi-finals, to become trainer, coach and assistant manager before succeeding Bill Shankly in 1974. In nine seasons as Manager he won six Championships, three League/Milk Cups, three European Cups, a EUFA Cup, a Super Cup, 6 Charity Shields, as well as being voted Bell's Manager of the Year six times. He retired in 1983. Paisley had played an important part in building the Liverpool team under the extrovert Shankly's leadership and when he became manager, he developed existing qualities and added style and sophistication to the team's play. He had a straightforward homely image but, nevertheless, possessed sufficient steel to ensure the club's place at the pinnacle of football. Whilst never possessing Shankly's charisma, he was greatly admired and respected throughout football and has earned a permanent place in Football's Hall of Fame. Made a Freeman of the City in 1983 and, in that year, became the first manager to lead his team up the Wembley steps to collect their medals, on his team's insistence, after their Milk Cup win against Manchester Utd.

PARROTT, John
Promising Liverpudlian snooker player. A winner of "Junior Pot Black" and maybe someone to challenge Steve Davis. A former pupil of New Heys Comprehensive School.

PARRY, Alan
Liverpool-born "Match of The Day" football commentator, and sports broadcaster who started his career with Radio Merseyside.

PATTEN, Brian
Poet, born in Liverpool in 1946. His work has been translated into many languages and he has received rave reviews for his childrens' books. Most notably "Mr. Moon's Last Case", which won an award from the Mystery Writers of America Guild. His collaboration with McGough and Henri in the 1960's earned him considerable popularity as one of the Liverpool Poets.

PAVILION THEATRE
The "Pivvy" in Lodge Lane, a famous Music Hall and Variety Theatre. Some of its old full-house patrons tried for full houses of a different kind when it was converted to a Bingo Hall. Sadly, it burned down in 1986.

PEEL, John
Merseyside's John Ravenscroft, now a top Radio 1 DJ after starting off in the 1960's with the pirate station, Radio London. Influential in promoting many 'underground' bands to wider audiences. Has been known to attend the occasional Liverpool FC match and all his children have LFC connections in their middle names, two are called Anfield, one Shankly and one Dalglish.

PENNY LANE
This rather ordinary Liverpool thoroughfare achieved immortality with the Beatles' brilliant song of the same name. The "shelter in the middle of the roundabout" is still there but the banker, nurse, fireman and barber may take a little more finding.

PETERS, Mary
Olympic pentathlon gold medalist at Munich in 1972, and for many years manager of Britain's women athletes. She was born in Halewood, Liverpool of Liverpool parents but hopped, stepped and jumped to Northern Ireland when she was twelve.

PETTIT, Sir Daniel E.A.
Chairman POSTEL Investment Management (formerly Post Office Superannuation Fund) and Olympic Games' footballer. He represented Great Britain in the 1936 Berlin Olympics. Born in Liverpool, 19 February, 1915, and educated at Quarry Bank High School, he was a director of Lloyds' Bank and was made a Freeman of the City of London, 1971.

PETTY'S, Harry
Famous old Liverpudlian restaurant selling cheap but good lunches. Many of Liverpool's office boys, including the young Tommy Handley, made their eating-out debuts at Harry's.

PHILHARMONIC
The Hall, Orchestra, Pub
All devoted to the spiritual fulfillment of Liverpudlians.

PHILHARMONIC
Royal Liverpool Philharmonic Society and Orchestra. The Society, one of the oldest in the world, was founded in 1840 and the Orchestra is the only major one in Britain with a permanent home of its own, the acoustically-unrivalled Philharmonic Hall.
The Society's first musical director was Max Bruch and other principal conductors have included: Charles Hallé, Henry Wood, Thomas Beacham, Malcolm Sargeant and Charles Groves.
Concerts at the Hall usually have an annual average attendance of around 90% and the Orchestra, which received its royal accolade in 1957, has frequently performed abroad, on radio and on record.
The Merseyside Youth Orchestra, affiliated to the Society, was formed in 1951.
Libor Pesek will become principal conductor and artistic adviser of the RLPO from September 1987.

The RLPO on tour at Ford's canteen in Halewood in 1984.

PHILHARMONIC
Hotel
"The most ornate pub in Britain", on the corner of Hope and Hardman Streets. A magnificent example of Edwardian flamboyance and style. The crystal chandeliers, friezes, copper panels, and carved mahogany were fashioned by the finest of craftsmen. Even the gents' urinal is a work of art.

Three members of the RLPO at an April Fools' Day concert in 1959. Are they trying to make the Guinness Book of Records? If so, don't tell Whitbread.

PICTON, Sir James

Surveyor, city councillor, author — "Memorials to Liverpool" — he was largely responsible for the lobbying for the provision of public libraries, and instrumental in the founding of the first in Duke Street. The library in William Brown Street and a road in Wavertree are named after him.

PIERHEAD

The location of Liverpool's world-famous waterfront, the buildings of the Royal Liver, the Cunard Building, and Mersey Docks and Harbour Co. headquarters. The site of the Liver Birds and many notable monuments. In recent years a rather ugly bus station has been added but the recent development of the Maritime Museum and Albert Dock Village has restored the area to one of great interest and visual impact. The famous ferries still leave for their short river crossings and, in summer weather, hundreds of office workers are attracted to the open spaces for lunchtime invigoration.

PITT STREET

Street that once formed the heart of the oldest "Chinatown" in Europe.

PLAYHOUSE THEATRE

The longest-running repertory theatre in Britain opened as the New Star Music Hall on 26 December, 1866, a most attractive building in Williamson Square. The list of 'names' who learned their craft there is impressive . . . Lillian Braithwaite, Cecil Parker, Clive Brook, C. Aubrey Smith, Michael Redgrave, Diana Wynyard, Rex Harrison, Robert Donat, Anthony Hopkins, Richard Briers, John Gregson . . . and that's just the chorus.

The Pope arrives at Speke Airport and the wind send his skull-cap flying.

POPE JOHN PAUL II

The Pope arrived at Speke Airport on 30 May, 1982, and travelling in the famous Popemobile, went first to the Anglican Cathedral where he was greeted by Bishop Sheppard. Accompanied by Cardinal Hume and Archbishop Worlock, the Pope entered the West Door and walked to the Nave Altar to the sound of great applause. The choir sang a Polish carol and the Pope thanked the choir master and organist, Ian Tracey, before giving a short blessing. The procession then proceeded along the street called Hope to the Metropolitan Cathedral. 18-year old Peter Scott of Childwall formally welcomed the Pope and John Cullen presented His Holiness with a memento made by the boys of St. Kevin's School, Kirkby. After communion, prayers and blessings, the Pope left amidst great excitement and spent that Sunday night at Archbishop Worlock's house in Allerton. The following morning the Pope left for Speke to continue his tour of Britain. It was estimated that over a million people had seen the Pope on his short but memorable visit to Liverpool. Catholics and Protestants together had rejoiced over the visit of this most charismatic of men.

The Pope blesses a disabled follower outside Archbishop Worlock's house.

PORT SUNLIGHT

The famous "Garden Village" created by William Lever, the great soap manufacturer. A magnificent example of town planning, incorporating a range of different styles of housing . . . including a replica of the row of half-timbered houses in Stratford-on-Avon where Shakespeare was born. The largest building in the village is the Lady Lever Art Gallery and Museum, one of Britain's finest private collections with paintings by Turner, Gainsborough and Reynolds, and Millais's portrait of Tennyson. Oriental pottery and porcelain are also noteworthy. There is a library, school, hotel, swimming pool, clubs and a war memorial to the memory of almost 500 Lever employees who were killed in the First World War.

POTATO FAMINE

The principal reason why so many Irish immigrants arrived in Liverpool during the 1840's. In 1847 some 300,000 Irish immigrants arrived, many to work as railway navvies.
It cost 6d. to cross the Irish Sea, in vessels that were termed "coffin" ships. At the time of the excavations for the Mersey Tunnel many attempted to dig their way back!

PUMP HOUSE

The most exciting pub development in 1987 will be the conversion of the 1870's Pump House which stands at the entrance of Albert Dock. Whitbread are converting the former hydraulic pumphouse into a pub . . . retaining the principal features but creating ground and mezzanine bars and forming a beer garden on the quayside.

Mass at the Metropolitan Cathedral.

His Holiness with Archbishop Worlock and Cardinal Hulme.

QUARRY BANK SCHOOL

At the time when two Labour Ministers, Shore and Rodgers, were serving, the school was dubbed 'Eton of the Labour Party' in recognition of their two political Old Boys.

QUEUE

The first reported queue in Liverpool was in 1895 for theatre tickets, insisted upon by the management of the Royal Court Theatre. It is difficult to find earlier reports of queuing anywhere.

QUIZ

Merseyside has long been associated with quiz leagues, and more informally any night out in a pub with a group of people often involves at least one pertinent brain teaser, either for humourous content or otherwise. It was a team from Merseyside Quiz League that won the BBC's inaugural "Masterteam" TV quiz in 1985. Hopefully, the quiz below will test, tease and tantalise.

1 Which King established Liverpool as a borough and a port in 1207?
2 Where in Liverpool could you see the portrait "Viscountess Folkestone" by Gainsborough?
3 Which Liverpool pub exhibits a sign "Emigrants supplied"?
4 What significant Merseyside event happened at 6 a.m., 21 October, 1974?
5 What was the name of the drummer who replaced the indisposed Ringo on the Beatles' world tour in mid-1964?
6 Who was the first Liverpool FC player to captain England?
7 Which famous Liverpool citizen was Allerton Hall once the home of?
8 TV comedy series set in Liverpool, which starred Paul Barber, Philip Whitchurch, Jean Heywood, etc . . . What was its title?
9 Which Liverpool park has duplicates of the famous London statues of Peter Pan and Eros?
10 Which Liverpool store was once the venue of Welsh National Eisteddfodau?
11 Which Liverpool theatre was the first in the country to be lit by electricity?
12 What Merseyside group had their first Top Twenty entry with "Messages" in 1980?
13 Which is the fence following the Canal Turn at Aintree Race Course?
14 By what name was Lime Street formerly known?
15 Where was the largest workhouse in Britain located in the nineteenth century?
16 A chairman of Everton for 17 years, he became President of the Football League. Who was he?
17 He wrote hit records for Mac and Katie Kissoon and was responsible for Liverpool FC's Top Twenty hit. A Liverpudlian . . . who was he?

18 Complete this sequence:
Sheila's Cottage . . . Russian Hero . . . Freebooter . . . Nickel Coin . . . Teal . . . Early Mist . . . ?
19 Local architect responsible for India Buildings, Martin's Building and the new Philharmonic Hall. Who was he?
20 Fighting Harada beat a well-known Liverpool boxer in a world title fight. Whom did he beat?
21 Who are the missing players from Everton's 1966 FA Cup winning team? West, Wright, Wilson, _____, Labone, _____, Scott, Trebilcock, Young, _____, Temple.
22 Who got 'six of the best' on his competitive return to Liverpool in the Autumn of 1977?
23 i) When was the Slave Trade abolished?
ii) In what year was slavery abolished in Great Britain and the Empire?
iii) In what year was slavery abolished in the United States of America?
24 Who is Mitzi Meuller?
25 Iris Caldwell was the sister of a well-known Liverpool beat star of the 1960's. She married Alvin Stardust/neé Shane Fenton, neé Bernard Jewry. Who was her brother?
26 Name the lady artist who has painted (not literally) many of Liverpool's most distinctive pubs?
27 Who succeeded Charles Groves as principal conductor of the 'Phil in 1977?
28 In which year did BBC Radio Merseyside begin broadcasting?
29 Which Archbishop of Liverpool first used the term 'A Cathedral in our time'?
30 What was the name of the Liverpool merchant who first broke the news that the Spanish Armada had set sail in 1588?

Tiebreaker:
What was 6LV and who was "Auntie" Muriel?

Your picture clue to Question 25 is shaking hands with a Young Frank Carson.

Answers to SCOUSEOLOGY QUIZ on Readers' Reply Page at the back of this book.

What are the following queues for?   Answers on Readers Response Page at the back of the book.

1 Parker Street, Liverpool, December 1946

2 Byrom Street, Liverpool, December 1946

3 Liverpool, April 1949

4 20 January, 1949

5 4 January, 1954

6   30 May, 1955

7   21 May, 1955

8   28 July, 1956

10   30 July, 1978

9   16 September, 1960

R

RATHBONE, Family
One of Liverpool's most famous families, the original William arriving in Liverpool in 1730. There followed several generations of William — five in total — all of whom played significant roles in the business, political and social development of the City. Early Rathbones were founders of the Society for Abolition of the Slave Trade, and William 3 (1757-1809) the first person to import cotton to Britain from the USA. William 4 (1787-1868) was an MP and social reformer who laid the foundation stone at St. George's Hall. William 5 (1819-1902), another MP, instrumental in the development of district nursing and the creation of the University of North Wales. On his funeral wreath Florence Nightingale wrote, "One of God's best and greatest sons".

Eleanor Rathbone

Eleanor Rathbone . . . no, they didn't call the girls, "William" — was the first woman councillor in Britain, one of the first women MP's and the first woman Minister of the Crown. She fought for much of her parliamentary life to introduce the Family Allowance system. She died in 1946.

RATTLE, Simon
Born in Liverpool in 1955, this brilliant conductor left the Royal Liverpool Philharmonic Orchestra to become Principal Conductor with the City of Birmingham Symphony Orchestra in 1980. Has been principal guest conductor of the Los Angeles Philharmonic since 1981, but has remained with the CBSO despite offers from many of the world's leading orchestras.
He was the winner of the Bournemouth International Conductors' competition when aged just 19.

RAWSTHORNE, Noel
Distinguished organist and resident at the country's biggest church organ in Liverpool Cathedral between 1955 and 1980 when he became Liverpool City Organist. Born in Birkenhead, 24 December, 1929, he was educated at Liverpool Institute. He has toured Russia and the continent and given many recitals for the BBC. Senior lecturer, St. Katherine College of Education, Liverpool. He was succeeded by Ian Tracey at Liverpool Cathedral.

RAY, Ted
Charlie Olden was, in fact, born in Wigan but arrived in Liverpool when a few weeks' old in 1909, and attended junior school at the same time as Colin Hunt's mum before going on to Liverpool Collegiate School. A keen sportsman, he was once on Liverpool's books as an amateur. His stage name came from the golf world, the famous golfer, Ted Ray. He played the Halls as "Nedlo the Gypsy — Fiddlin' and Foolin'", an act which interspersed comedy and violin playing à la Jack Benny. It was radio, however, that was to provide his niche and he became one of radio's greatest funny men. He initially made an impact in 'Calling All Forces', written by Bob Monkhouse and Denis Goodwin, in which he acted as compére. The show produced a classic catchphrase which became a nationwide hit. "You should use stronger elastic" was Ray's reply and his invention, to any number of statements referring to falling down, dropping down etc. etc. Among his early foils were Diana Dors and the then unknown Marilyn Monroe. But it was the show, "Ray's A Laugh", which established him as a great radio comic. A natural raconteur, his sons, Andrew and Robin, also found fame. He died in 1977.

RAY'S A LAUGH
The show which was responsible for Ted Ray's fame started in 1949, lasted eleven years and was a must for Light Programme listeners around Sunday lunch-hour. Ray, more or less playing himself, with a radio wife, Kitty Bluett, coming into contact with a variety of famous characters, Mr. Trumble, Sydney Mincing, Al-K-Traz, Mrs. Easy, Tommy Trafford, and Crystal Jellybottom to name but a few. Many of the shows catchphrases were nationally used:
"What's your name little girl?" "Jen-ni-fer"
"He's looverly, Mrs. Hardcastle — he's looverly" and
"It was agony, Ivy, agony".
The supporting cast was impressive — Peter Sellers, Dick Emery, Graham Stark, Patricia Hayes, Pat Coombs, Kenneth Connor, Charles Hawtrey, Bob and Alf Pearson, John Hanson and Fred Yule all appeared in the show — talented support to Ted Ray's sharp wit, delivered in a low-key style reminiscent of some of America's comedy legends.

RAYMOND Paul
Real name Geoffrey Anthony Quinn. Liverpudlian entrepreneur famous for his "Revue Bar" and "Men Only".
He was Manufacturers' Association Tie-Man of the Year in 1975.

REAL THING
Liverpool group with distinctive American "soul" sound. Their first hit "You to Me are Everything" made No.1 in 1976 and they followed this up with two other Top Ten hits: "Can't Get by Without You" and "Can You Feel the

Real Thing (left to right): Ray Lake, Eddie Amoo, Chris Amoo and Dave Smith

Force?''. Well worth a listen is their album ''4 from 8'' which also has a stunning Liverpudlian sleeve. ''You to Me are Everything'' and ''Can't Get by Without You'' were re-released in 1986 and again reached the Top Ten.

REDDING, Dr. Stanley Gordon
Liverpool has the oldest Chinatown in Europe and, possibly as a result, has produced someone such as Dr. Redding. Based at the University of Hong Kong, this former employee of Owen Owen is now one of the world's leading authorities on China.

REDMOND, Phil
Liverpool-born creator of TV's ''Grange Hill'' and ''Brookside'' and joint founder of Mersey Television. ''Brookside'' broke new ground as a soap opera in dealing with many of the relevant issues of the day and, despite early controversy, ''Grange Hill'' developed into a popular and significant children's TV landmark. The cast of ''Grange Hill'' recorded the anti-drug song ''Just Say No'' in 1986. Redmond's most recent TV series is ''What Now?'' set in Liverpool and featuring post-school teenagers in modern Britain.

RED RUM
The greatest Grand National horse ever and a big favourite. Trained by Ginger McCain in Southport, the horse won the World's toughest race in 1973 and 1974 ridden by Brian Fletcher, and then, in one of Aintree's most emotional moments, won again in 1977, this time ridden by Tommy Stack. Since retirement, has been in great demand for opening garden fetes, etc. A bronze statue has been commissioned for Aintree.

REECE, Brian
Liverpool actor, member of the well-known milk and confectionery firm, best known for his radio role as P. C. Archibald Berkeley-Willoughby in the ''Adventures of P.C. 49''. The series started on 24 October, 1947, and the last episode of the tenth series was broadcast on 26 May, 1953 (The Case of The Small Boy). Reece's well known catchphrase from the series was ''Oh, my Sunday Helmet''.

Brian Reece

REECE'S
Well-known Liverpool milk and confectionery firm with a major store in Clayton Square over which was the famous restaurant and ballroom. Among the many who chose the restaurant for their wedding breakfast was John Lennon, after his marriage to Cynthia Powell.

REES, Nigel
Born in Liverpool in 1944 and educated at Merchant Taylors, he devised Radio's "Quote, Unquote" and wrote the very successful "Graffiti" series of books.

REMEDIOS, Alberto
Born in Liverpool of Spanish parents in 1935, he was a Queen's Prize winner at the Royal College of Music and his tenor tones have since been heard in many of the world's great opera houses as well as the Kop at Anfield. This one-time Cammell Laird's welder played for New Brighton FC before transferring his affections to Liverpool FC. Bill Shankly was one of the guests when he featured on "This is Your Life".

REYNOLDS, Gillian
TV, radio presenter and critic, on programmes such as Face the Press. She introduced a special Womans Hour from her home city for Radio 4 in July 1986.

RICHMOND LEGH
1772-1827. Born in Liverpool, educated at Cambridge University, he was ordained in 1798. He wrote a series of religious tracts with moral themes under the title, "Annals of the Poor". The first in the series, "The Dairyman's Daughter", was translated into 19 languages, and over 4 million had been circulated by 1849.

RIGBY'S
Dale Street, old and atmospheric City centre pub. There was an agreement in the 'Nelson Room', signed by Nelson himself, for the supply of his favourite Marsala wine to be shipped to the Fleet off Malta. It was stolen in 1976.

The Rockin' Robbins.

RIGBY, Eleanor
Title of a Lennon and McCartney song — one of their most poignant — and also the title of the statue, sculpted by Tommy Steele and donated to the City of Liverpool as a tribute to the Beatles, in 1982.

Tommy Steele's tribute to the Beatles . . . and his gift to the City. The gravestone in St. Peter's, Woolton, which inspired the song. But would Eleanor Woods have made the same impact?

ROBBINS, Kate
Paul McCartney's cousin who had a No.2 hit "More Than In Love" in 1981.

With sisters Emma, Amy and Jane, and with a little help from brother Ted, she starred in a TV variety show called "Robbins" in 1986.

ROBINSON, Anne
Former Liverpool Echo writer from Blundellsands who stood in for Barry Took on BBC TV's "Points of View" in September 1986 and appears regularly on Breakfast TV. An assistant editor with the Daily Mirror, she becomes the permanent host of "Points of View" in 1987.

ROBINSON, Bernard
Liverpudlian, responsible for starting the Marie Curie Foundation in Britain.

ROBINSON, John
The Liverpool actor, educated at Holt School, and another Playhouse 'old boy', best known for his role as Quatermass in the 1953 TV serial.

ROBINSON, Joseph Armitage
1858-1933. Theologian and historian, he was Dean of Westminster Abbey, 1902-11, and awarded KCVO, 1932. Educated at Liverpool College.

ROBINSON, Robert
"Call My Bluff", "Ask the Family", "Stop the Week" are just three of the TV and radio programmes that this Liverpool-born intellectual is well-known for.
His publications include "The Dog Chairman", "Landscape with Dead Dons" and "Inside Robert Robinson".

RODERICK, Ernie
Liverpool boxer who was British Welterweight champion for nine years from 1939. He fought the great Henry Armstrong for the World Title in 1939, but lost on points over 15 rounds. He was briefly British Middleweight champion, and married Nel Tarleton's sister, Edna.
A European title-holder, he was the first boxer to be the recipient of the British Boxing Board of Control's £1 per week pension, for winning a Lonsdale Belt outright. He died, aged 72, in June 1986.

RODGERS, Bill
The Rt. Hon. William Thomas Rodgers was one of the "Gang of Four" (with Jenkins, Owen and Williams) who left the Labour Party on the formation of the SDP, becoming Vice-President in 1982. Educated at Quarry Bank High School, he was Secretary of State for Transport, 1976-79.

RODNEY STREET
Well-known City centre thoroughfare off Mount Pleasant, frequently referred to as "Liverpool's Harley Street". Gladstone, Monsarrat, Brian Epstein, Hugh and Anne Clough were born in the street.
The 19th century biographer, Lytton Strachey, who published a biography of Queen Victoria, lived in the street whilst at Liverpool University.

ROSCOE, William
1753-1831. The distinguished Liverpudlian who could claim to be the City's most talented and versatile son. Author, poet, painter, botanist, lawyer, banker, Member of Parliament, etc., etc. His most famous literary works include "Life of Lorenzo de Medici" and "Leo X". Many of his collection of paintings are now housed in the Walker Art Gallery including Simone Martini's "Christ discovered in the Temple", painted in 1342. He was responsible for the Botanical Gardens in Mount Pleasant, and had the courage of his convictions in being a strong opposer of the slave trade, and active among the Liverpool abolitionists. More than anyone else, Roscoe was responsible for a new interest in Italian art and culture at the time, and earned himself an international reputation.

ROSSINGTON, Norman
Liverpool-born light-comedy actor who has appeared in many films and TV programmes. Born Liverpool, 24.12.1928, educated at Sefton Park Elementary School, began work as an office boy on the docks. Original member of the cast of "Salad Days". Films include "Saturday Night and Sunday Morning", "Hard Day's Night" and "Tobruk".

Norman Rossington with you-know-who during the making of 'Hard Day's Night'.

ROSSITER, Leonard

He played two of television's most brilliant comedy characters in the 1970's, Rigsby in "Rising Damp" and Reggie Perrin in "The Rise and Fall of Reginald Perrin". Born in Liverpool in 1926 and educated at Liverpool Collegiate, this former insurance salesman had developed into one of Britain's best stage actors by the time of his sudden and premature death in 1984. His stage credits included "Arturo Ui", "The Heretic", "The Caretaker" and films "A Kind of Loving", "Billy Liar", "2001", "Oliver" and "Brittania Hospital", etc. He spilled a considerable amount of Cinzano over Joan Collins in one of TV's best-known commercials.

ROUTLEDGE, Rev. Canon Kenneth

Canon and Treasurer, St. Paul's Cathedral, since 1982. Born 1927 and educated at Birkenhead School and Liverpool University, he was called to the Bar in 1952. He was an unsuccessful candidate for Birkenhead in the 1959 General Election.

ROUTLEDGE, Patricia

Actress and singer born in Birkenhead, educated at the High School and Liverpool University. Her first stage appearance was at the Playhouse in 1952 and her London debut in 1956 in "The Duenna". For her performance on Broadway in "Darling of The Day", she received a "Tony" award for Best Musical Actress, 1967. Countless stage and TV roles followed and she has also made many films, "To Sir with Love", and "30 is a Dangerous Age, Cynthia", included. She appeared on TV in the very funny Victoria Wood series.

ROYAL IRIS

In its heyday, cruising up and down the Mersey on Saturday nights rivalled the Stadium for the number of fights it staged. In recent times, the image has changed, but the bruises remain on many of its passengers from those earlier days.

Rossiter as Rigsby in 'Rising Damp'.

ROZA, Lita

Liverpool's first No.1 Hit Parade chart-topper with her 1953 hit, "How Much is that Doggie in the Window", the first British girl singer to reach No.1 in the charts. Rumour had it that her sister worked at Gillies the Grocers in Belle Vale. Or was it Ted Ray's sister? Anyway, Lita was once the champion butter patter of Merseyside's Home and Colonial Stores before going on to sing with Ted Heath's great band.

Royal Iris

RUDKIN, Alan

Brilliant and stylish boxer who was British Commonwealth and European Champion. He fought three game, but losing, battles for the World Bantamweight title but did, however, win the biggest battle of all — as a youngster overcoming Perthes Disease, a hip disorder which left him with his left leg shorter than his right. He became a publican in his home city on retirement.

RUNCIE, Robert

The current Archbishop of Canterbury was educated at Merchant Taylors, Crosby, and is a supporter of Liverpool FC. With supporters in such elevated ecclesiastical positions, this may partly explain the club's stunning success over the past decade or two.
He served in the Scots Guards during the Second World War (awarded the MC) and was Bishop of St. Albans, 1970-80.

RUSH, Ian

World-class Welsh International striker with a Scouse accent almost in Jan Molby's class. He became Britain's costliest footballer in June 1986 when Liverpool transferred him to Juventus for £3.2 million. In a glittering five full seasons at Anfield he had the remarkable record of never scoring in a match that Liverpool lost (121 in total). In 1983/84 season he scored 49 goals (50 if you include the penalty in the European Cup Final shoot-out), was Footballer and Players' Player of the Year and European Golden Boot winner. He had an outstanding game in the 1986 Cup Final, scoring two goals in Liverpool's historic win and scored 4 goals in a derby game at Goodison on 6 November, 1982, when Liverpool won 5-0. A restriction on foreign players to the Italian League enabled him to have a final season at Anfield.

Rudkin victorious in his fight against Tsuganezawa at the Royal Albert Hall, 1967.

An Archbishop and a Bishop have breakfast in Toxteth, served by 8 years-old Karla Starkey.

Willy Russell in front of the Odeon Cinema, London Road, for the Merseyside premiere.

RUSSELL, Lord Russell of Liverpool

2nd Baron Edward Frederick Langley Russell. 1895-1981. Became world-famous with the publication of "Scourge of the Swastika" in 1954, an account of Nazi war atrocities. At the time he was Assistant Judge-Advocate-General, and when the Lord Chancellor indicated that the publication was incompatible with his judicial office, he resigned from the Law to concentrate on writing.

Educated at Liverpool College and Oxford, he was awarded the MC (plus 2 bars) for services in the First World War and was a Brigadier in the Kings' Regiment (Liverpool). He saw service in the Second World War and was made a Companion of the Legion D'Honneur in 1960. His other publications include, "The Knights of Bustido" about Japanese war atrocities, "Deadman's Hill — Was Hanratty Guilty?" (1965), and "The Trial of Adolph Eichmann".

His father was editor of the Liverpool Daily Post (1869-1919) and first President, Liverpool Reform Club.

RUSSELL, Willy

A playwright strongly influenced by his home city and currently one of British theatre's leading lights. He left school at 15 and became a hairdresser, writing songs and singing in folk clubs in his spare time. His first major stage success was "John, Paul, George, Ringo and Bert" in 1974 when Russell was 27. There followed several successful TV plays, "Our Day Out", "Daughters of Albion", "One for the Road", etc., before "Educating Rita" made him a major name. First performed by the RSC in 1980, Rita was a tremendous critical and popular success, winning three major theatre awards and a very successful film version followed. In 1983, "Blood Brothers" was first presented at the Playhouse Theatre, transferring to the Lyric in London, and then winning the Society of West End Theatres' 'Best Musical of the Year' award.

S

St. JOHN, Ian

Mersey soccer legend of the 1960's, signed for Liverpool FC from Motherwell in 1961. His "canonisation" by Liverpool supporters was immediate. He scored a hat-trick in his first game for the club, a "friendly" against Everton. His charismatic, skilful play endeared him to the Kop supporters who adopted the anthem, "When the Saints go Marching in", in tribute. A reply written on a church poster in Liverpool in the late 1960's summarised his legend. The poster asked, "What would you do if Jesus Christ came to Liverpool?" The handwritten answer: "Move St. John to inside-right".

A Scottish International, he scored the winning goal in Liverpool's first-ever FA Cup win in 1965. Now a TV soccer presenter, linking up skilfully with a bygone adversary, Jimmy Greaves. He still lives in the City.

St. NICHOLAS'S CHURCH

At the Pierhead, the Parish Church of Liverpool and the 'Sailors Church'. The weather vane is in the shape of a ship, an emblem of St. Nicholas, the patron saint of sailors. The church, originally founded in the 14th Century, was destroyed and rebuilt. The tower was replaced in 1815, the original tower being damaged when the spire collapsed on Sunday, 11 February, 1810, killing 25 people, including 19 girls from a local charity school in Moorfields. The bells are world famous as being amongst the finest rings.

In spite of most of the building being reduced to a blazing shell by German incendiaries on the night of 20th September, 1940, the west end tower and belfry remained untouched. Throughout the war the Church never closed its doors to the thousands of servicemen of all nations calling in for a few quiet moments before going to join the war.

SALT FISH

Traditional Liverpudlian Sunday breakfast delicacy. Excellent thirst guaranteed for the midday bevvy.

SAUNDERS, Ron

Liverpool-born football manager of West Bromwich Albion FC and former Everton player. He was Manager of the Year in 1975 and in 1981, when he won the Championship with Aston Villa, skippered by Liverpudlian Denis Mortimer. Saunders left for St. Andrews but Villa went on to win the European Cup, thanks to a winning goal by Peter Withe, another Liverpudlian. A centre forward, Ron Saunders scored over 200 league goals for Everton, Gillingham, Portsmouth, Watford, and Charlton in spite of being rejected by Tranmere Rovers because he was too small. His Uncle George was also an Everton player in the 1940's.

An active participant in combatting the problems affecting soccer and a campaigner for better standards.

SAYLE, Alexei

Since his great success as a cult comedian and social commentator at London's Establishment Club in the late

1970's and early 1980's, Liverpool-born Alexei — the son of Jewish Marxist parents — has received regular and increasing exposure on TV and films. His comedy cameo in the film, "Supergrass", is a perfect illustration of his talents.

SCAFFOLD

Roger McGough, John Gorman and Mike McGear formed the very popular pop and poetry group of the 1960's. "Thank you very much" (for the Aintree Iron) reached No.4 in the charts in 1967 and "Lily the Pink" was No.1 for four weeks at the end of 1968. They had their last top ten hit in 1974 with "Liverpool Lou".

SCALA, Gia

Actress born in Liverpool in 1934 of Italian and Irish parents, best known for her film performance as the allegedly dumb traitor in "The Guns of Navarrone". She died of an overdose in 1972.

SCOTT-ARCHER, Zena

of Scott's Detective Agency, Liverpool. She was the first woman President of the World Association of Detectives and the first woman President of the Association of British Investigators. A high-heeled gumshoe!

SCOTLAND ROAD

"Scottie Road", one of Liverpool's best known thoroughfares, much changed since the days when it boasted a pub on every corner and a 'chippy' within staggering distance of each pub.

SCOTT, Elisha

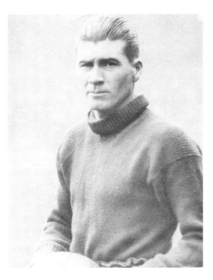

It is said that Liverpool's famous international goalkeeper of the 1920's was walking down a Liverpool street one day, when he spotted the great Everton goalscorer and his deadly rival, Dixie Dean, opposite. Dixie, renowned for his prolific heading ability, nodded towards Elisha, who instinctively dived in an attempt to save an imaginary ball. The argument has raged ever since as to whether he saved the ball or not.

SCOTT, Tom

Completed the Grand National course, jumping all the fences, in 1870. Oh yes, WITHOUT a horse. His son was to become a Mayor of Bootle.

SCOUSE MOUSE

Name of loveable new comic character created by George Nicholas. This character and his chums form the centrepiece of the world's longest continuous mural painted in a corridor at Alder Hey Children's Hospital in Liverpool. The mural (or 'muriel', as Hilda Ogden would say) is over ¼ mile long and covers a painted area of over 33,670 feet. It was painted by young people of Merseyside and is featured in the Guinness Book of Records.

The Scouse Mouse Trust Fund has raised over £1 million in funds for the hospital.

"Scouse Mouse" is also a title of part of George Melly's autobiography.

SCOUSER

The term, applied to natives of Liverpool, is derived from the traditional dish of the City.

Scandinavian in origin, lobscouse as it is called in the land of the Vikings, became popular as a low cost staple meal. The 'lob' got lost in the North Sea and variations of this culinary delight include "blind scouse" , i.e. without meat.

When taken in the correct ambiance the thick, soupy mix of meat, veg and potatoes is quite delicious, particularly when enriched by the inclusion of a pig's foot.

SCUFFERS/ROZZERS/BIZZIES

Liverpudlian nicknames for policemen.

SCUPHAM, Peter

Poet, born in Liverpool, 1933, and educated at Cambridge. His work, including "Prehistorics"(1975), "Hinterland" (1977), and "Summer Palaces" (1980) has received much critical acclaim.

SEARCHERS, The

Sixties Liverpool pop group who had three No.1 hits with "Needles and Pins" (1964), "Sugar and Spice" (1963), and "Sweets for my Sweet" (1963). Their name was inspired by the John Ford movie which starred John Wayne, and they were to the Iron Door Club what the Beatles were to the Cavern. Their original high-pitched vocal harmonies were performed by Mike Pender, John McNally, Tony Jackson and Chris Curtis.

The Searchers in New York, 1964.

95

Bill Shankly is embraced by tearful fans at the Charity Shield Match in 1974, shortly after his announcement of retirement.

SEDDON, Richard John

1845-1906. Born on Merseyside, he worked in a Liverpool foundry before emigrating to New Zealand, after first trying Australia, in 1866. Was elected to Parliament in 1879 and became Prime Minister in 1893, a position he held until his death, thirteen years later. A popular and famous figure, he was known as "King Dick", and introduced many progressive social reforms, including old age pensions.

SEFTON

The Molyneux family, one of the most important on Merseyside through the centuries, and at one time Constables of Liverpool Castle. The Earls of Sefton lived at Croxteth Hall until the death of the seventh Earl when the line ended and the Hall and grounds were donated to Merseyside County Council who ran the estate through the Museum Service until the abolition of the Council in 1986. The future is unclear but it is likely to be run through a Trust. The name lives on as a district of Merseyside, a park bigger than any of London's and a race at the Grand National meeting.

SEXTUPLETS or "The Waltons"

Hannah, Lucy, Ruth, Sarah, Kate, Jenny . . . born November, 1983, to Janet and Graham Walton of Wallasey, Merseyside. Britain's first surviving sextuplets and the world's first surviving all-girl sextuplets.

SHAFFER, Peter . . .

Born in Liverpool in 1926, this leading contemporary dramatist has had many critical and popular successes since his first play "Five Finger Exercise" ran for 607 performances in the West End in 1958. Amongst his other works are: "Royal Hunt of the Sun", "Equus" and "Amadeus", all of which were filmed. The film version of Amadeus won the Oscar for Best Film in 1985.

. . . and Anthony Shaffer

Twin brother Anthony is also a well-known dramatist best known for "Sleuth", an ingenious and popular stage success which was filmed with Laurence Olivier and Michael Caine, who were both nominated for Oscars in the same year that Marlon Brando won, and returned the award.

Both brothers have won "Tony" awards the prestigious Broadway Theatre prizes.

Anthony won for "Sleuth" in 1970/71 and Peter in 1974/75

for "Equus" and again in 1980/81 for "Amadeus".
Not a question of which twin wears the Tony for the Shaffers.

SHAKE HANDS
Name of character in Bleasdale's "Boys from the Black Stuff", played by Iggy Navarro. Despite a minor role in one episode of the series, achieved a cult following in Liverpool and has since been busy opening fetes, etc., and a stall in ITV's "Albion Market".

SHANKLY, Bill
Born in Glenbuck, Ayrshire, in 1913, his unwavering fanaticism for football matched him with just the right environment when he joined Liverpool FC from Huddersfield Town in 1959. For 15 years he managed the club and won the admiration and affection, not only of the Anfield followers, but of the whole football world. But it was on Merseyside that his adulation was most intense and by the time of his sudden death in 1981, he had become the most loved and respected sports personality in the City's history. His great qualities of enthusiasm, motivation and dedication were chiefly responsible for laying the foundations of the world-renowned football club that Liverpool has now become. Under his management, Liverpool won the 2nd Division Championship, the Football League Championship three times, the FA Cup twice and the EUFA Cup once. Among the players he managed were St. John, Hunt, Yeats, Clemence, Keegan, Callaghan, Toshack and Tommy Smith. He was a man of the people whose tough, swaggering charisma couldn't hide the warmth, humour and honesty that were always associated with the man.
His widow, Nessie, performed the unveiling of the Shankly Gates at Anfield, a permanent reminder at the ground of his unforgettable contribution to the club. His quotes were often very funny and outrageous.
When asked if he thought that football was as important as life and death he replied, "No, it's more important than that". Maybe in Liverpool in the 1960's he had a point.

SHARP, Jack
(1878-1938). Well-known sports shop in Whitechapel, its founder was a double England international at soccer and cricket. He played outside-right for Everton, Aston Villa and England. As a middle-order batsman, fast-medium bowler and brilliant cover fieldsman he played 518 matched for Lancashire between 1899-1925, captaining them in his last two seasons. He played in three Tests for England in 1909, scoring one century (105).

SHAW, Frank
Ex-customs officer who wrote with knowledge and affection for his home city, including "You know me Aunty Nelly" and "My Liverpool", published in 1971, the year of Frank's death. Ironically, this archetypal Scouser, one-time Jesuit novice and Hoover salesman, was born in County Kerry but moved to Liverpool as a youngster.

SHEILA'S COTTAGE
The Liverpool Estate Agent had finished taking the details of the house that was to go on the market when he turned to the vendor saying: "It's a very nice house and a nice gesture to name it after your wife". The vendor smiled, "My wife's called Doreen" he replied "The house is named after the horse that won the deposit for me".
Sheila's Cottage won the 1948 Grand National at 50-1.

Sheila's Cottage wins the Grand National

SHEPPARD, Rt. Rev. David
Aptly named, this Bishop of Liverpool has tended to his Scouse flock since 1975. In this soccer-crazy city, the Bishop's cricketing pedigree loses some of its glamour. During a career stretching from 1947-1963, Sheppard captained Cambridge University, Sussex and England, for whom he played 22 times. He gave a moving and much-publicised Dimbleby Lecture in 1983 on Inner-City deprivation, which drew greatly on his Liverpool experience. A former Bishop of Woolwich.

SHIRLEY-QUIRK, John
Leading bass-baritone, born in Liverpool, 28 August, 1931, and educated at Holt School and Liverpool University. A professional singer since 1961, he has toured Europe, Australia, Israel and made his first appearance at the Metropolitan Opera in New York in 1974. Awarded a CBE.

SHORE, Peter, MP
Labour Shadow Cabinet Minister and former Minister in the Wilson/Callaghan Cabinets. Shore was educated at Quarry Bank High School, a distinction he shares with John Lennon (former lead singer with the Quarrymen). Peter Shore also went on to join a noisy group — The Fabian Society.

SILVERMAN, Sidney Samuel, and LIVERPOOL in the 1930's

Labour MP and capital punishment abolitionist, Sidney Silverman was born at 46 Hardwick Street, Liverpool, on 8 October, 1895. The street, now demolished, was in the Brownlow Hill/Pembroke Place area. His father was a Jewish immigrant from Rumania who had arrived in Liverpool when he was 16, attracted by its cosmopolitan and racially-tolerant image. He became a credit draper, although Sidney's background was never affluent and he was one of the first to win a free scholarship to the Liverpool Institute, after originally attending Vine Street Wesleyan School in preference to the local Jewish school. Silverman was a bright scholar, earning the nickname, 'Quicksilver', at the Institute, and eventually he received a First Class B.A. degree at Liverpool University. During the First World War he spent two years in jail as a conscientious objector and used that time to read, endorsing his Socialist views, and reading his favourite authors, Shakespeare, Browning, and George Meredith. He accepted a post as lecturer in English Literature at the University of Finland in Helsinki, teaching there for four years before returning to Liverpool University to take Law. A First Class degree followed and he started a law practice at 81 Dale Street in January 1928.

He soon gained a reputation as a working man's lawyer and some of his better-known cases vividly recreate Liverpool's history in the 1930's. He successfully defended a client who was alleged to have thrown a brick at Oswald Mosley during a political rally in Liverpool, rendering him unconscious. He also defended his friend and political ally John Braddock, husband of Bessie. Braddock was charged with inciting a riot during an unemployment march in Islington, Liverpool, in

Silverman with Nye Bevan at Beaconsfield, Bucks in May 1954, defending him on the charge of dangerous driving.

1932. Braddock maintained he was in the Kardomah café at the time of the riot, despite eye witnesses giving evidence to the contrary. The Counsel for the Prosecution was David Maxwell Fyfe. The case was lost and Braddock sentenced to

Electioneering in Liverpool 1933.

six months' imprisonment despite Silverman's intensive and careful work on the case, and E. G. Hemmerde's skilful interpretation of his instructions. An appeal was lodged and Silverman produced new evidence for the hearing and for Sir William Jowitt and E .G. Hemmerde who represented Braddock. David Maxwell Fyfe again represented the police. The appeal was successful and Silverman and Braddock returned from London to be greeted by a large cheering crowd at Lime Street Station. Braddock had served a month of his sentence and whilst in jail, Silverman had helped him in his Council election campaign to return him as Councillor for Everton. The Town Clerk had to visit Walton Jail to swear Braddock in as a member of Liverpool City Council.

On another occasion, Silverman successfully defended a client who maintained that he had been manhandled in police custody. Selwyn Lloyd (later to be Chancellor of the Exchequer and Foreign Secretary) was briefed by Silverman, and their opposition counsel was again Maxwell Fyfe. Selwyn Lloyd had also been Silverman's acting barrister on the Mosely case.

Meanwhile, Silverman's political career was developing. He was elected to the City Council to represent the St. Anne's Ward, an area which had some of Britain's worst housing and social conditions. He narrowly lost a Parliamentary by-election in Liverpool Exchange. His opponent was Colonel Shute, Conservative, a well-known businessman with a distinguished war record, and a Roman Catholic. The division had a large Catholic population and religious allegiance had a more significant bearing in the Liverpool of the 1930's.

He married Nancy Rubenstein, a renowned cellist and member of the well-known musical family, at Hope Street Synagogue in 1933 and eventually, in 1935, was elected MP for Nelson and Colne, a seat he was to hold until his death in 1968. Silverman had long been opposed to capital punishment. He had published "Hanged and Innocent" in 1953, and his lobbying was rewarded when, in 1964, his Private Member's Bill for complete abolition was mentioned in the Queen's Speech, the first in history to receive this accolade. When the Bill reached the Lords, its chief opponent was . . . David Maxwell Fyfe, now Lord Kilmuir, his old Liverpool adversary.

The eventual abolition provided Silverman's finest hour, but shortly afterwards the country was shocked by the horrendous Moors murders, which took place a few miles from Silverman's constituency. As a consequence, one of Silverman's opponents in the 1966 General Election was Patrick Downey, an uncle of one of the Moors victims who stood solely for the re-introduction of capital punishment. In a much-publicised contest, Silverman was returned.

A colourful and controversial character, and one of Parliament's leading back-benchers, his uncompromising views on Socialism probably denied him high political office and at one time led him to expulsion from the Parliamentary Labour Party. An active member of CND, Chairman of British Section World Jewish Congress, his opposition to capital punishment could be likened to Wilberforce's opposition to slavery. After several strokes, one during Question Time at the Commons — when he was carried out by Tom Swain only to return after recovering in the lobby — the five-foot tall dynamo died on 9 Feburary, 1968.

SISSONS, Peter
ITN Newscaster who has appeared on same Liverpool Institute school photographs as Paul McCartney and George Harrison.

SLATER, Larry
Petty Officer Aircrewman. Modern day hero who has saved countless lives working for the Royal Navy's Rescue Service. He was responsible for rescuing Simon Le Bon of Duran Duran when lowered from the RN's helicopter to pick up Le Bon and five other crew members of the yacht 'Drum' during the Whitbread 'Round the World Yacht Race' in August 1985. Earlier that same day he had rescued nine other people in stormy seas off the Cornish coast.
Born in Wavertree, Liverpool, 1953, and brought up in Anfield, he was educated at Rathbone Primary and John Hamilton schools. He was awarded the George Medal and the subject of a 'This is Your Life' when he met his own hero . . . Kenny Dalglish.

SMITH, Geoff
Liverpool distance runner who won two Boston Marathons and was second in the 1983 New York Marathon.

SMITH, Herbert Tyson
Local sculptor whose work can be seen on the external friezes of the magnificent Martins building in Water Street. Worked for some years from a studio in the Bluecoat, and was an inspiration to many local artists. He was also responsible for Liverpool's Cenotaph at St. George's plateau.

SMITH, John
Chairman of Liverpool FC and of the Sports Council. His wise and unobtrusive leadership of Liverpool FC over the past decade or so has played a significant part in the emergence of the club as one of the world's most famous teams. Awarded the CBE.

SMITH, Neville
Actor/writer who, with Gordon Honeycombe, was responsible for the BBC TV play "The Golden Vision" set in Liverpool and with a title inspired by Everton's gifted centre forward Alex Young. Wrote and appeared in "Gumshoe" starring Albert Finney, which also used Liverpool for its location.

SOLOMON, Samuel
Super salesman who lived in luxury in Liverpool from the profits of his magic medicine — the 'Balm of Gilead'. The tonic sold at eleven shillings — for 'internal problems' if drunk, and cured 'weak and shattered constitutions'. When rubbed on it could act as an aphrodisiac. Solomon had over 400 agencies in Britain, 16 in America and others throughout the world. For all its considerable powers in the nineteenth century, it was eventually discovered that the 'balm' was nine parts undiluted brandy!

SPEKE
District of South Liverpool which houses Liverpool Airport, Speke Hall and the mammoth council housing estates built in the post war years. The airport, opened by the City Council in 1933, was one of the most sophisticated in the world,

incorporating many of the new technical advances and earned a reputation for its safety in landings.

Speke Hall, a magnificent black and white half-timbered Tudor mansion owned by the National Trust, was built by the Norris family and completed in 1598. The Norris family continued their allegiance to Roman Catholocism after the Reformation, and built their own chapel within the house. The priest's holes, an interesting feature of the house, were built in order to hide the priests when necessary. The Hall has a life-size painting of John Middleton, the famous Childe of Hale. He lived between 1578-1623 and was a 'mere' 9 feet 3 inches in height and is mentioned in Pepys' Diary. There is a pub of the same name in the attractive nearby village of Hale, and his king-size grave is in Hale churchyard.

The council estates were developed as a result of Liverpool Corporation's success in attracting new factories to Speke in the 1930's, including Dunlop, Bryant & May, and Evans Medical.

Paul McCartney once lived at 12 Ardwick Road, Speke, and his father was at one time the secretary to Speke Horticultural Society.

Liverpool Airport's new ultra-modern terminal became operational in April 1986, incorporating a rapid transit service with domestic passengers with hand-luggage able to move from plane to their cars in less than three minutes. In 1987 it is anticipated that the new British Aerospace A.T.P. aircraft will make its world debut on the Liverpool to London route.

SPIEGL, Fritz
Austrian-born Liverpudlian (by his own adoption). Musician, writer and broadcaster. Creator of cultural events and commentator on folklore. Although music is his primary career, his publishing achievements include: "Lern Yerself Scouse" (65), "Liverpool Ballads", "The Liverpool-Manchester Railway" (70), "A Small Book of Grave Humour" (71). Formerly principal flautist with the Royal Liverpool Philharmonic.

SPINNERS, The
Renowned folk group who were household names at the Cavern years before the Beatles. Tony Davis, Mick Groves, Cliff Hall, and Hugh Jones combine to present songs and ballads that are romantic, raunchy, rowdy, bawdy, salty and sad. From the people, by the people and for the people.

SPIRIT
As epitomised by courageous 9 yr old Jamie Baker, the brave Evertonian who led his team on to the field at Goodison Park against Manchester United in September 1986, and who died from leukaemia that night. His story touched everybody and the Echo instigated the Jamie Baker Memorial Trophy, to be played annually between the Football Supporters' Associations of Liverpool and Manchester.

The 'Spirit of Merseyside', a replica of a 19th Century Liverpool pilot cutter, left Albert Dock on Friday, 24 October 1986 on its maiden voyage, manned by unemployed Merseyside young people.

STADIUM, The
The only purpose-built boxing hall in Britain, situated in Bixteth Street and opened in 1932. The new Stadium replaced the Pudsey Street Ice Rink which had staged major boxing promotions since 1911.

The Stadium was built on the site of an old graveyard and, together with the fact that many title-holders came to grief there, gave the hall its nickname of the 'graveyard of champions'. Hopefully the death-knell hasn't sounded on this historic and famous boxing venue.

and LIVERPOOL BOXING
It was Arnold Wilson who first promoted boxing at Pudsey Street in 1911 and Liverpool has long enjoyed a reputation as a major British boxing area. Strangely, the only local boxer to hold a world title is Kirkby's John Conteh, who beat Jorge Ahumada to win the Light Heavyweight crown at Wembley on 1 October, 1974. However, countless British, European and Commonwealth crowns have been won by Merseyside's boxers. The first major fight to be held at Pudsey Street was the British Bantamweight Championship on 14 September, 1911, when Digger Stanley beat Ike Bradley on points over 20 rounds and, a month later, Sid Smith beat Louis Ruddick to win the British Flyweight title.

Among the best known Merseyside boxers have been: Conteh, Nella, Ernie Roderick, Volante, Stan Rowan, the McAteers — Pat and Les — who were both middleweight champions, Rudkin, Tommy Molloy, Johnny Cooke, Joey Singleton, Alf Howard and Birkenhead's Wally Thom, a British and European Welterweight champion before becoming a famous referee. He died in 1980. Gus Foran, Billy Ellaway, Billy Aird, Martin Hansen, and Keith Wallace are other notable names. Tony Willis, an Olympic medalist, won the British Lightweight title in 1985, and in the same year Ray Gilbody became bantamweight champion. Two World Flyweight titles have been won in Liverpool by British boxers. Percy Jones of Porthcawl won on 26 March, 1914, and Peter Kane of Golborne beat Jackie Jurich on points on 22 September, 1938. The distinguished careers of Hogan 'Kid' Bassey, Dick Tiger and Joe Bygraves — who beat Henry Cooper for the Commonwealth title — were closely followed on Merseyside as they were based in Liverpool. Merseyside's Lonsdale Belt winners are Tarleton, Roderick, Rudkin, Thom, Pat McAteer, and Singleton. Nel Tarleton holds a unique record that cannot be emulated. He is the only boxer to have won a National Sporting Club belt (the original) and a British Boxing Board of Control belt. Jimmy Price, now a professional light-heavyweight, won a Commonwealth Games Gold as a middleweight in 1982 and London-based Liverpudlian Rocky Kelly was the opponent of Steve Watt, who tragically died a few days after their contest in London in March 1986. Watt had been in a coma for several days.

STARR, Freddie
One of Liverpool's most outrageous and talented contributions to British show business. Despite a controversial career, he remains one of the biggest attributes to the country's theatre's and clubs. His impersonation of his idol, Elvis, is a classic, and only he could get away with a 'visual' Ray Charles impersonation.

Originally fronted 'the Midnighters' during the Mersey beat boom of the sixties. As a pop singer, reached No. 9 in the charts with the 1974 hit, "It's You".

STARR, Ringo

Richard Starkey, born 9 Madryn Street, Dingle, 7 July, 1940. Replaced Pete Best as the Beatles' drummer. Pete was better-looking, Ringo was a better drummer. Ringo had previously earned a reputation as drummer with Rory Storm and the Hurricanes and, at the suggestion of George Martin, Brian Epstein invited him to join the Beatles a month or so before recording "Love Me Do" on 4 September, 1962. The decision was not popular with Beatles' fans at the time, but Ringo went on to become a loveable and humorous member of the 'Fab Four'. When the group split Ringo continued his recording and film career. He had already starred in several films, most notably "The Magic Christian" and "Candy". He married Maureen Cox, a Liverpool hairdresser, in February 1965, and is now married to American actress, Barbara Bach.

STEADMAN, Alison

Brilliant Liverpool actress she won the prestigious Evening Standard Best Actress Award in 1977. Probably best-known for her tour-de-force in 'Abigail's Party' both on stage and on TV. Married to Mike Leigh, she has also appeared as a comedy actress on radio in programmes such as 'News Huddlines' and Eddie Braben's "The Show with Eight Legs".

STEEL, Alan Gibson

The first Liverpudlian to captain the England cricket team, he captained them for four tests including three in 1886 when England won each match. He played for Lancashire and once took 9-63 against Yorkshire at Old Trafford (1878), a season in which he took 164 wickets at 9.43 and scored 537 runs (at 22.37). His three brothers Douglas, Ernest and Harold, also

Freddie Starr "auditioning" for Hot Gossip.

born in Liverpool, all played for Lancashire and Douglas was a Cambridge Blue at cricket, rugby, and soccer. Allan's son, Allan Ivo, also played county cricket for Middlesex but was tragically killed in action in 1917 in Belgium.

STEER, Phillip Wilson

1860-1942. Artist born at Birkenhead and member of Liverpool Academy. On returning from France his versatile and original paintings gave cause for him to be dubbed "Constable's successor". The Arts Council sponsored exhibitions of his work in 1986 at the Fitzwilliam Museum Cambridge, and at Stoke, Bradford and Newcastle.

STEWART, Ed

Radio DJ and presenter whose support of Everton FC started after being taken to a match as a youngster. Chelsea beat Everton 6-0 that day, but his support remained loyal and has been rewarded with the Club's recent staggering successes.

STILGOE, Richard

Merseyside-influenced wordsmith who was educated at Liverpool College and has been a regular feature of the entertainment scene for some years. He once played on the same bill as the Beatles, playing lead guitar with Tony Snow and the Blizzards. Bernard Falk was the groups rhythm guitarist. Playwright, poet, musician, lyricist, presenter, collaborator . . . what next?

STIRLING, James Frazer

Internationally acclaimed architect, born in 1926 and educated at Quarry Bank, Liverpool School of Art and Liverpool University School of Architecture. He is the winner of many awards, including the American Reynolds and Brunner prizes and the Pritzker Prize. His work includes Runcorn New Town housing, redevelopment of West Mid-Town Manhattan for New York Planning Commission, the History Faculty at Cambridge University and the Harvard University Museum. Other work in Berlin, Stuttgart and Iran. Featured in BBC/Arts Council film and was consulted by the United Nations for low cost housing projects in Peru.

STORER, Harry (Jnr.)

Born in West Derby, Liverpool, the son of Harry (Senior) who played soccer for Liverpool. Harry Junior played for Derby County and England (2 caps, 1925 & 1928), became a football manager, and as a county cricketer played 302 games for

Yoko Ono and Sean Lennon on a visit to Strawberry Fields in 1984.

Derbyshire between 1920-1936.

A great character, when he was a football manager he once invited one of his players to take a walk over the pitch with him after a match. Storer, his head down looking at the pitch, was eventually interrupted by the player, "What are you looking for Boss?" he enquired. "The hole you hid in all afternoon". Storer replied.

STORK

Nom-de-plume of Joe Wiggall, an authoritative writer on boxing, soccer and racing for the 'Liverpool Echo' until 1958. His successor on boxing matters, Syd Dye, is still reporting on the local boxing scene.

STRAWBERRY FIELDS

A Salvation Army childrens' home near to where John Lennon lived with his Aunt Mimi and Uncle George. The title of a haunting Lennon song of 1967 and a Stephen Poliakoff 1977 stage play. The name given to a section of Central Park, New York, a memorial to Lennon, where over 120 governments have planted a tree for peace.

STUBBINS, Albert

Liverpool FC centre forward of the immediate post-war years. Highly accomplished forward who was unlucky not to get a regular England place. His face appears on the LP sleeve, "Sgt. Pepper's Lonely Hearts Club Band", just to the right of Beatle George.

STUBBS, Rt. Rev. Charles William

1845-1912. The Church's involvement in radical political activity is not new, as evidenced by this Liverpool-born theologian and social philosopher confirms. Educated at Liverpool Institution School and Rector at Wavertree (1888-94), his published works include:
Christ and Democracy, For Christ and City (Liverpool

Sermons), The Land and the Labourers, A Creed for Christian Socialists, Charles Kingsley and the Christian Social Movement. A select preacher at Cambridge University (1881-95), he was appointed Bishop of Truro in 1906).

STUBBS, George

1724-1806. Liverpool-born painter, considered to be the greatest of all animal painters. His works, "Molly Longlegs" and "Horse Frightened by a Lion" can be seen in the Walker Art Gallery. He was briefly apprenticed to Hamlet Winstanley at Knowsley Hall.

STUDHOLME, Marion

ARCM. Principal soprano Sadlers Wells Opera Company, 1949-1960, Merseyside-born and educated at Childwall Valley High School.

SUTCLIFFE, Stuart

Talented painter, his work was shown at John Moores Exhibitions and his murals adorned the Jacaranda Club in Slater Street. He met John Lennon at Liverpool Art College and played bass in the early days of the then Silver Beatles. He stayed on in Hamburg after meeting Astrid Kirchheer but died, tragically from a brain tumour on 10 April, 1962.

SWIFT, Clive

Born Liverpool, 9 February, 1936, he joined the RSC in 1960, and has an extensive list of film and TV credits to his name. Was married to writer Margaret Drabble.

SURTEES, Allan

Liverpool-born actor, 1924, who was a tea boy, rent collector and draughtsman before going into show business. His film credits include: "The Reckoning", "Ten Rillington Place", and "Get Carter". He played Colwyn Stanley in TV's "The Brothers McGregor".

T

TALKING STREETS
BBC Documentary broadcast in 1958 reflecting the opinions of people living in the back streets of Liverpool.
Liverpudlians Frank Shaw and Stan Kelly worked on the programme, which was produced by Denis Mitchell, later to earn a reputation as one of the country's foremost documentary film-makers.

TALL SHIPS RACE
A highlight of the 1984 Garden Festival was the visit to the Mersey of the magnificent sailing ships taking part in the Cutty Sark Tall Ships Race. The ships started to arrive in the Mersey on 1 August and a carnival atmosphere prevailed in the City as thousands came to see the ships arrive, visit the Maritime Museum and take the ferry to Vittoria Dock in Birkenhead to see the ships berthed.
There was a march-past of the sailors to the Philharmonic Hall and the Orient Express made a special journey, arriving at Lime Street Station.
The ships left the Mersey in the early evening of 4 August, and provided a memorable and unforgettable sight as hundreds of thousands lined both sides of the Mersey to witness a fitting climax to a magical Merseyside event.

TARBUCK, Jimmy
Born 1940, achieving meteoric fame as a cheeky comedian 20 years ago in the early days of the Beatles, Liverpool-born Tarbuck has now matured into one of Britain's best-known comedians. Hosted the highly-popular "Sunday Night at The London Palladium" when his topical gags where performed to the backcloth of Tarby's Wall. He has appeared regularly on television ever since and accomplished a successful run of live Sunday night variety shows. Almost as well-known for his golfing prowess and his support of Liverpool FC, the likeable Tarbuck is at his best as a raconteur.
Followed fellow Liverpudlians Frankie Vaughan, The Beatles, and Derek Nimmo as Variety Club's Personality of the Year in 1985. Attended Dovedale Road School and St. Francis Xavier's.

TARLETON, Nel
Affectionately known as 'Nella', one of Liverpool's and Britain's most accomplished boxers. He was British Featherweight champion and Lonsdale belt holder, and successfully defended his title when he was almost forty years old. He twice fought Freddie Miller, the American, for the world title. At Anfield in 1934 and at the Stanley Track in 1935, but lost narrowly both times. His achievements were all the more remarkable as he had only one lung. A great stylist who fought frequently in his home City, he died in 1956. His permanent place in Liverpool folklore is assured as he is the subject of the well-known Mersey quiz question: "Who was the last man to box Tarleton?". The answer? "Coyne, the Undertaker".

TATE, Henry
After discovering a new way of cutting sugar in a Liverpool factory, he opened a factory of his own (which has gone) and eventually gave his name to a gallery in London (which is still there).

TAYLOR, Prof. Laurie
Liverpudlian Professor of Sociology at York University. A regular broadcaster, particularly on Radio 4's "Stop the Week".

TAYLOR, Philip Meadows
1808-1876. Novelist/historian born in Liverpool of Anglo/Indian parentage. He wrote a massive trilogy beginning with "Tara", chronicling 200 years of Indian History, and also "Confessions of a Thug" (1839) an investigation into Thuggee in India. He was for many years a "Times" correspondent.

TEARDROPS ON MY DRUM
Title of fascinating autobiography by Jack Robinson, published in paperback in 1986, which contains evocative descriptions of Liverpool life in the 1920's.

THELWELL, Norman
Born in Birkenhead on 3 May, 1923, he attended Liverpool College of Art and worked as a clerk in Liverpool. One of Britain's most popular cartoonists, particularly with his observations on country life. A regular contributor to Punch, his many cartoon anthologies include 'Angels on Horseback', 'Thelwell Country', 'Compleat Tangler', 'This Desirable Plot'.

THETIS, HMS
The ill-fated Cammell Laird built submarine which sank during trials in Liverpool Bay on 1 June, 1939. 99 lives were lost, the worst submarine tragedy ever. She was later recovered, renamed HMS Thunderbolt, and was finally sunk in the Mediterranean in 1943.

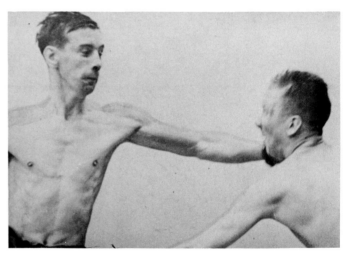

Tarleton (left) in action against Ivor Drew at Wrexham in 1936.

THOMAS, Brandon
Born in Mount Pleasant, Liverpool, in 1856. Wrote "Charley's Aunt" in 1892, his one real success. It has been translated into 22 languages including Zulu and since it opened in 1892 it is claimed that there has not been a single week when it has not been performed somewhere in the world. He could have written a sequel called "Son of Charley's Aunt" but, no doubt, had difficulty working out that relationship.

THOMPSON, Phil
Liverpool-born footballer, has captained Liverpool FC and England and has a collection of championship and cup medals. Is credited as the first footballer to use the standard interview reply "Sick as a parrot", though has had a career in which, for the most part, he has been "over the moon". He returned to the Anfield coaching staff from Sheffield United in July 1986.

NO HOPE"—THETIS A CL

MEN DEAD IN THE WORST
SUBMARINE DISASTER

Men Believed Victims Of Vessel's Escaping Chlorine Gas

SPERATE RESCUE WORK FAILS

---

mmell Laird's Statement On What Is Thought To Have Happened

RTLY AFTER THREE THIS AFTERNOON AN FFICIAL OF CAMMELL LAIRDS TOLD WAITING RESSMEN, " WE HAVE NOW NO HOPE OF SAVING URTHER LIVES FROM THE THETIS.'

consider that the men died from chlorine gas. The ship rried a large quantity of chlorine, which we think would cape owing to the angle at which she lay."

denied that there was any truth in a suggestion that they were ntemplating blowing the vessel up. Now that there was no hope saving life, the official said, they would attempt to save the ssel.

y-eight men have lost their lives.

Admiralty stated this morning that following tappings eard at 2 a.m. there was still hope at 10 a.m. to-day that me of the trapped men might be rescued alive.

, however, faded as the hours sped by with no news that e vessel had been brought to the surface from her position the seabed 14 miles off the Great Orme's Head.

late this afternoon, an official of Cammell Lairds told the Press at hope was abandoned prior to midnight. He added, concerning e tapping said to have been heard at 2 a.m., that it was now ought to have been due to high compressors working.

FIC TASK

fic task faced the salvage workers who at dawn began a new tempt to raise the stern of the submarine. The first attempt failed, e hawser parting, and although the workers then realised that the ances of rescuing the trapped men were remote they continued ving desperately to raise the submarine.

additional names of men aboard, announced by the Admiralty -day, show that there were 102 men on board the Thetis when she de her fateful dive. Four of these escaped, so the number of prisoned is 98.

hout a night of increasing anxiety relatives and friends of the pped men kept a sad vigil at the Birkenhead offices of Messrs mmell Lairds, the builders of the Thetis. As time wore on menfolk broke down under the strain and the ambulance staff was lled to render first aid.

f the four survivors have been brought back to Merseyside. eutenant Woods is now in the Southern Hospital, Liverpool, suffer- from nervous exhaustion and shock. Mr. Frank Shaw, a Cammell rds fitter, returned to his home, 31 Ivydale Road, Birkenhead,

---

Before All Hope Had Gone

The last that was seen of the submarine before her stern vanished bene the waves.

A.R.P.
PROBLEMS

Special pages in the DAILY POST of Monday will deal with air raid precaution problems as they affect both the private person and the employer of labour, and will provide a useful guide to meeting Government requirements' and recommendations.

Monday's
DAILY POST

DRAMA INSIDE
SUBMARINE

Plan Of Escape For Men

WATERTIGHT MESSAGES

In Case First Men Out Were Not Saved

DAVIS CUP TENNIS

HARE RETIRES IN GAM AGAINST GERMANY

C. E. Hare, showing signs of suffering from the trouble which e made him a doubtful starter, surren to Menzel in the Britain v. Ger Davis Cup (European zone) semi in Berlin this afternoon.

He played only two sets, losing first 6-love and the second 6-1 i. exhibition that can only be describ pitiful.

Germany now leads Britain b/ match to nil.

WIRRAL TENNIS

The Wirral tennis tournament continued on the Hill House cour Heswall this afternoon. Results:—
OPEN MIXED DOUBLES
(First Round)
P. O'Connell and Miss B. O'Connell beat W. and Miss D. Beck, 6-1 6-0.
MEN'S HANDICAP DOUBLES
(Semi-final)
S. J. Armstrong and G. P. Harris (owe 3/6) b Platt and W. Law (30), 6-1 6-1.

WINDSOR RACING RETURN

2 0 —SPEEDY PLATE of £200 two res Five furlongs.
9 3 Mr P Baldin's TULLYFORD...R Perry
Stork's Selection
8 7 Mr E Gwilt's Redpoll.............S W
8 4 Mrs Benson's Maid of Windsor.Cliff Richa
8 7 Mr W Barnett's Harvest Feast...T Bart
8 7 Ld Abergavenny's Green Croft Colt
R Rathb
8 4 Miss Ella Atherton's Co-Star....T P Bo
8 4 Mr R Anthony's Peter Pan.......R Ru
8 4 Mr P Beary's Mountain Cloak.....M Be
8 4 Lord Carnarvon's Patty ....G Richa
8 4 Mr T H Farmloe's Harqueen.......J K
8 4 Capt Hedley Hughes' Cloudburst Filly
J O'Gr
8 4 H.H. Aga Khan's Miss Rustom...W Rick
8 4 Mr G P Parry's Lady Sonia Gelding.K Gr
8 4 Mr Arthur Sainsbury's Penmead..H Pack
Winner trained by T E Leader
Betting—7 to 4 agst TULLYFORD and Has 9 to 2 Redpoll 10 to 1 Patty, Miss Ruston Mountain Cloak, and 20 to 1 any other.
Tote (including 2/ stake)—Win, 6/3; 2/9, 5/1, 23/5.
Won by two lengths; length and a half, going one furlong Patty slipped up and Richards was thrown.

2 30 —CASTLE SELLING HANDICAP of £200 One mile.
Off at
7 7 11 Mr S Wootton's GONG..........
7 7 Mr C Jarvis's Mountain

Bigger than Blackpool's.

THRELFALLS
Famous old Liverpool brewery that has played a part in local folk lore.
"What are yer doing for yer holidays?"
"Going to the Falls".
"Oh yeah, Swallow or Niagara?"
"No, Threlfalls".

TICKLE, THE MISSES
Listing from a mid-fifties Liverpool telephone book.

TIDY, Bill
Prolific cartoon contributor to 'Punch' and many other periodicals, and a regular guest on TV and radio panel shows, etc. Creator of the Fosdyke Saga, Bill was once a useful footballer with Essemay Old Boys.
He won the Granada Television Press Award for Best Cartoonist in 1973.

TITANIC, The
The most famous ill-fated ship of maritime history was a White Star liner, registered in Liverpool, and there were many Merseysiders among crew and passengers when the ship sank on 14 April, 1912, with 1,513 lives lost. We may have to wait until the Titanic is raised and let the ships log put an end to one of the Mersey's greatest mysteries, namely, did the Titanic ever visit Liverpool or was it her sister ship, The Olympic, as most people believe?

"TOFFEES"
The nickname of Everton FC. Toffee was first made in Everton over 200 years ago, at Molly Bushell's house in Everton Brow.

TOMPIAN, Thomas
1629-1713. Famous Liverpool clockmaker renowned for the world's first spring-driven grandfather clocks. Tompian was one of a number of illustrious Liverpool 17th century clockmakers which included Lassell and Aspinwall.

TOPHAM, Mirabel
Strong-willed former "Queen of Aintree" who was owner of the course until 1974. She was briefly a West End actress. She died in 1980.

TOWER
New Brighton's famous structure was the highest in Britain when built between 1897-1900 — 621 ft, 120 ft higher than Blackpool's. As a result of neglect in maintenance during the First World War it was demolished in 1919.
A Merseyside playground, the resort built the biggest open-air swimming pool in Europe, and Britain's biggest promenade and indoor amusement arcade. There are plans to revitalise the resort.

TOWN HALL
The City's third, designed by John Wood has survived fire, cannon (during a seamen's protest in 1775), a Fenian attempt to blow it up in 1881, and war damage in 1941. It still remains one of Liverpool's most distinguished buildings, with civic suites to match any in the country, an example of Georgian excellence.

LAST SPORTING EDITION.

"TITANIC" DISASTER.

EBERG STRUCK IN MID-ATLANTIC.

MMOTH LINER STILL AFLOAT.

O LOSS OF LIFE FEARED.

PASSENGERS ALL TAKEN OFF.

"VIRGINIAN'S" TIMELY RESCUE.

egrams received early this morning that the new White Star liner , which left Southampton on Wed- on her maiden voyage to New York, en in collision with an iceberg last

first telegrams gave the sensational that the liner was sinking; then long silence, in the course of which vest fears were felt; but later in the welcome news was circulatec that nce had reached the damaged vessel, at there was no danger of loss of

eassuring statement was issued from w York office of the White Star Line afternoon that the Allan liner an was standing by the Titanic, and ll the passengers had been safely off.

messages stated that the damaged as slowly making for Halifax, N.S.; e report from New York declares he liner, which is badly damaged d, is sinking.

news of the accident was sent by from the Titanic, which at the as in 41.46 N. lat., 50.14 W. long.

essel reported that immediate assist- as required, and that she was sink- the head.

umber of passengers on the Titanic she left Queenstown, including the rg passengers, was: First class, cond class, 305; third class, 800; with and stewards numbering 903; or a n board of 2,358.

g the passengers are Mr. Bruce managing director of the White ne, and Mr. J. J. Astor.

vessels which got into wireless com- tion with the Titanic were the an, the Baltic, and the Olympic, l sped to her assistance.

al liners report an enormous icefield Great Banks of Newfoundland. The liner Niagara, which has arrived York, was extensively damaged by r the spot where the Titanic col- ith a berg.

Titanic, which belongs to the White Line, is the world's largest ship, a tonnage of 46,382, or 1,004 more he Olympic.

s under the command of Comman- ward J. Smith, who had been trans- from the Olympic.

Titanic is insured for £1,000,000, but valued at £1,500,000. Fifty-five guineas nt. was quoted for reinsurance this on.

t of the Titanic's saloon passengers on Page 7, and a picture, descrip- the vessel, and chart showing the n of the ship at the time of the is given on Page 4.

SENGERS TAKEN OFF

DANGER OF LOSS OF LIFE.

following telegram was received fternoon concerning the Titanic

the liner Baltic has also reported herself within 200 miles of the Titanic, and says she is speeding to her help.

The last signals from the Titanic came at 12 27 this morning.

The Virginian's operator says that these were blurred, and ended abruptly. —Reuter.

REPORTED SINKING.

New York, Monday, 3.45 a.m.—A telegram from Cape Race at 10.25 Sunday evening says:—"Titanic reported she had struck an iceberg. The steamer said that immediate assistance was required. Half-an-hour afterwards another message was received saying that the Titanic was sinking by the head, and that the women were being taken off in lifeboats."—Reuter.

New York, Monday (later).—A telegra.. from Cape Race says the wireless telegraph operator on board the Titanic reported that the weather is calm and clear, the position of the liner being then 41.46 N., 50.14 W.

The Virginian at midnight was 170 miles west of the Titanic, and is expected to reach her at ten o'clock this morning.

The Olympic at midnight was in 40.32 N. lat., 61.18 W. long. She is also in direct communication with the Titanic, and is hastening to her.—Reuter.

"UNSINKABLE."

New York, Monday.—Mr. Franklin, vice-president of the White Star Company, while admitting that he was without recent information, announced that the Titanic was unsinkable.

The fact that she was reported to have sank several feet by the head was unimportant. She could go down many feet at the head as the result of water filling the forward compartments, and yet remain afloat indefinitely.—Exchange telegram.

NEWS IN LIVERPOOL.

The publication of the news in Liverpool caused the greatest alarm. Anxious inquiries were made at the White Star

and reports having run through the pack on Thursday afternoon. She sustained no actual damage, although she was in grave danger for a time.

The passengers say they sighted twenty-five icebergs, one cluster, indeed, no further than a hundred feet away. The liner had to feel her way through an ice lane for hours.

The French liner Niagara did not escape unscathed. She was holed twice beneath the water line, and had some of her plates buckled. At a given moment a wireless telegram was sent from her to the Carmania for assistance, but later the captain decided that he was able to navigate the ship to port without help, having temporarily repaired the damage to the Niagara's hull.

The steamers Kura, Lord Cromer, and Armenian, which arrived here during the last few days, also report having had a dangerous experience, and having sustained more or less damage by ice. It is known also that at least one full-rigged ship and one fishing smack are imprisoned in floes.—Press Association Foreign Special.

THE RESCUE SHIP.

The Allan liner Virginian, which has been mentioned in connection with the disaster to the Titanic, is a turbine triple-screw steamer of 12,000 tons. She is 540ft. in length, and 60ft. broad. The Virginian, with her sister ship the Victorian, was the first ocean-going liner to be equipped with the Parsons turbine engine. She carries the long distance Marconi apparatus, which has proved of such signal service on the present occasion, and was one of the first liners to publish a daily newspaper on board. She has a speed of about 19 knots, and is one of the fastest vessels in the Canadian service.

The Allan liner Virginian left Halifax for Liverpool at nine o'clock on Saturday night.

QUESTION IN COMMONS.

Mr. Buxton announced in the House of Commons, this afternoon, that he had received a telegram from the White Star stating the only information they had received was contained in a telegram from New York as follows:—"Newspapers' wireless report Titanic collision iceberg. Women put into lifeboats. Steamer Virginian expects to reach the Titanic ten to-day."

HOME RULE.

MR. BALFOUR'S ATTACK.

NO FAIR AND SQUARE ISSUE.

COUNTRY NOT CONSULTED.

The debate on Mr. Asquith's motion for leave to introduce the Home Rule Bill was resumed in the House of Commons, this afternoon, by

Mr. Balfour, who, on rising, was received with loud cheers. He said he heard Mr. Gladstone introduce his first Home Rule Bill in 1886, amid scenes of unprecedented parliamentary interest. While he did not intend to dwell upon the past, he thought the House should mark the changes in political situation since then and the profound changes which had come over the policy which Mr. Gladstone's successors now propounded. The first Home Rule Bill was defeated by the secession of the most distinguished members of the Liberal Party, and the result was a permanent division. Those who supported Mr. Gladstone, in his next Government, came pledged either cheerfully or reluctantly to carry any scheme of Home Rule he might produce. The result was that there was no serious division in the ranks of the party, and it was left to the second chamber to reject the bill and for the country to endorse its action. It was with

THESE TWO LESSONS

behind them that the party in power had approached the question. They had learned two things—that the people of this country left to themselves had no love for this separating and dividing policy. The moral of that was that they ought never to bring this question as a fair and square issue. before the electorate at any time and in any circumstances. Never since 1892 had it been

STOP-PRESS EDITIO

EXCITIN DOCK SCENE.

A horse and cart fell into the Clarenc Dock this afternoon. The horse wa drowned.

PENDLEBURY RIOTS.

Five colliers were charged at Man chester to-day with rioting and assaulting the police on the 6th inst., when the police and colliers came into contact at Pendle bury.

BILLIARDS.

Interval.—Diggle (in play), 1,667; Inma 808.

Interval.—Harverson 2,180. Reece (in play) 2,127. Breaks: Reece 96 and 137 Harverson 41.

COMMERCIAL.

Chicago, 9.40 a.m.—Wheat: July ⅛c. down.

New York Cotton. — 11.45 a.m call: May 11.12, July 11.18, Oct 11.27, Jan. 11.33. Steady.

New York Stock Exchange, 11 a.m (Special Cable to George Smith and Co.) Union Pacific 171⅜, Canadian Pacific 252, U.S. Steel 70⅝, Amal. Copper 81⅜. Tone Irregular.

Chicago Board of Trade, 10.30 a.m (special cable to Geo. Smith & Co.). Wheat unchanged (strong), corn ⅜ down (strong), lard 2½ down, ribs 2 up, pork unchanged, hogs 5 u (steady). Hog receipts, 37,000.

London Stocks.—Markets closed irregularly. Consols kept their advance. Hom Rails rose ¼ to ⅜. Americans harde Rubbers off colour.. Oils very firm Mines harder in places.

Liverpool Stocks. — Latest Prices of Americans: Union Pacific 176⅛ ⅜. U.S Steel 72⅛ ⅜. Canadian Pacific 258⅜ ⅜ Trunk 27 11-16 ⅜, Third Pref. 59½ ⅜.

THE TITANIC.

An official message from New Yor confirms the report that the Titanic making for Halifax under her own steam

Twenty boat loads of the Titanic's pa passengers have been transhipped on the Allan liner Parisian, and others on t the Cunarder Carpathia.

HOME RULE BILL.

Mr. Balfour said Ireland had now mor than her full share in the control of th House of Commons.

He believed the Government's idea Ireland as the "poor relation" was alto gether wrong. He wished to know wh would have control of the constabulary The margin allowed the Irish Executiv would lead to customs barriers bein created between Ireland and Gre Britain.

THE TITANIC.

Wireless messages from Cap Race says the Virginian is towin the Titanic.

IRELAND'S M.P.'S

Mr. Asquith stated in the House

TOXTETH

Until the 16th century the area was stocked with deer, which provided food and sport for the hierarchy of Liverpool. The Dingle marked the site of a stream which ran down what is now Park Road and past the Ancient Chapel of Toxteth. At the time of Liverpool's great social and economic growth, many of the non-conformist, Unitarian families set up home in the area, and in 1867 the development of Sefton Park commenced, resulting in one of the biggest and best public parks in Britain. The district became better-known as Liverpool 8, and in the 1960's was at the centre of the cultural and artistic Liverpool scene. The riots of 1981 gave the area a new national image and the media's attention has been intensive ever since. As a result of the disturbances, Michael Heseltine led a deputation of business leaders to the area and he became, for a while, "Minister for Merseyside", making positive attempts to revitalise the area and seeking means of reducing the deprivation.

TRAMS

Europe's first continuous tram service, designed by American inventor, George Train, was started in Birkenhead on 30 August, 1860, and ran between Woodside and Birkenhead Park via Shore Rd, Argyle St. and Conway St.

Liverpool's last tram, a No.6a, took its last journey in September 1957.

Affectionately known as "Green Goddesses", the trams ran on tracks which have now formed natural dual carriageways in some suburbs of the City.

In October 1986, Ron Jones a Merseyside Tourism executive and author of "The American Connection" launched a crusade to return Liverpool's last tram to the City. He had visited the Trolley Museum in Maine, USA, where he discovered the tram had been neglected for many years, after having been sold for £100!

TRANMERE ROVERS FC

Merseyside's third-ranking soccer club, but the second oldest, having been founded in 1883. Although never achieving the heights of their illustrious neighbours, Rovers have had a loyal following since their entry into the Football League in the old Third Division North in 1921. They were promoted to Division II in 1938 but, unfortunately, relegated after just one season. Their place in the record book is fairly secure, however, as they were the leading participants in the Football League match with the most goals. The match took place on Boxing Day 1935, when they beat Oldham Athletic 13-4, their centre forward 'Bunny' Bell scoring nine . . . and he missed a penalty. Bell's individual record was beaten by Joe

'Bunny' Bell holds the ball after scoring nine against Oldham.

Payne, of Luton, four months later when he scored 10. Bell was a prolific scorer for Tranmere, 104 goals in 114 games, and he eventually left the Prenton Park club to understudy Tommy Lawton at Everton. Another Tranmere 'Bell', Liverpool-born Harold, is one of the Football League's most regular performers. He played 595 games for the club between 1946-1964, and went nine seasons without missing a league match (a record). The club survived extinction a few years

'Pongo' Waring scores against Millwall at Prenton in August, 1938.

ago and are currently enjoying a mini-revival in Division Four. Although attendances at Prenton have never been massive there is absolutely no truth in the rumour that Lord Lucan has been hiding in the stands this past decade or so.

TREBILCOCK, Mike

Everton were two goals down in the 1966 FA Cup Final against Sheffield Wednesday, when two goals from this little-known Cornishman brought them back into the match. They eventually went on to win and so complete one of football's greatest comebacks. Little was heard afterwards of Trebilcock, but his one performance that afternoon at Wembley made him a Mersey soccer legend. Needless to say, his name has been the inspiration of a Liverpudlian story or two (or even three).

TREBLE

Liverpool FC made history in 1983/84 when they became the first Football League club to win three major competitions in one season. They won the League Championship (for the third consecutive season), the Milk/League Cup (for the fourth consecutive season, also a record), and the European Cup. Joe Fagan was Manager of the Year, Ian Rush won the Player of the Year, the Player's Player of the Year, and the European Golden Boot. That season the City completed a unique clean sweep as Everton won the FA Cup and the FA Youth Cup. Liverpool Reserves also won the Central League title. London, Manchester and Birmingham complained to the European Court for a fairer distribution of football trophies!

TRESSELL, Robert

The pen name of Robert Noonan, the house painter of Irish ancestry who wrote "The Ragged Trousered Philan-thropists". The book first appeared in 1918 but in 1955 was republished in a fuller version. The story of corruption, hypocrisy and exploitation has become a classic text of the Labour movement. Its author died of tuberculosis in Liverpool in 1911 and was buried in an unmarked pauper's plot in Walton Park cemetery, just 50 yards from the walls of Walton Gaol, unrecorded until the unveiling of a monu-ment to his memory in 1977.

TROJANS

The Liverpool Trojans baseball team were formed in 1946 and have won the British championship three times. Their grounds have included Everton FC's training ground at Bellefield and Bootle Stadium.

TUNNELS

The longest underwater road tunnel in the world when completed in 1934. The Queensway Tunnel was officially opened by King George V in July 1934 and ran 2.13 miles (or 2.87 miles including branch tunnels), linking Liverpool with Birkenhead. The total cost was £7.75 million. The rock and debris which resulted from the excavations was dumped at Otterspool and the City Council decided to develop the site as a riverside promenade and park.

This tremendous enterprise resulted in the promenade being opened to the public in 1950, and aroused world-wide interest in its conception and completion. An original proposal for a promenade had come from J. A. Brodie in 1919.

A second Mersey tunnel, 'Kingsway', linking Liverpool with Wallasey was completed and opened by the Queen in 1971.

A further example of Liverpool "tunnelling" took place in the early 19th century, when Joseph Williamson the 'Mad King of Edge Hill' — organised a labyrinth of tunnels in the area, seemingly for no purpose but to provide work for the unemployed.

TURNER, Peter

Liverpool actor and author of "Film Stars Don't Die in Liverpool", the story of his relationship with the glamorous Hollywood actress, Gloria Grahame. She was the star of movies such as "Oklahoma", "The Big Heat" and "Not as a Stranger". She spent the last week of her life in Sefton Park before flying back to New York where she died of cancer hours later. The book has already attracted six screenplay offers! (Published in 1986).

TUSHINGHAM, Rita

The elfin-faced Liverpool actress was just 19 when she shot to fame in her first film, "A Taste of Honey" in 1962, a per-formance which won her Best Actress Award at the Cannes Film Festival. Roles in "The Knack", "The Girl with Green Eyes", and "Dr. Zhivago" followed. The ex-convent girl, now a Muslim after her second marriage to Ossi Rawi, lives in Canada but returns regularly to see her family in Liverpool.

TYSON, Cathy

Everyman-trained Liverpool actress who, for her first film part, was chosen to be Bob Hoskin's leading lady in 'Mona Lisa' in 1986. On stage, she played Miranda in 'The Tempest' at the Barbican. She is married to contemporary Liverpool poet, Craig Charles.

U

UGLY FACE CLUB OF LEVERPOOLE

Existed in Liverpool between 1743-1753. It is not known whether its disappearance was the result of lack of members or over-subscription.

UNIVERSITY

Liverpool's University was founded much later than it would be imagined, partly because many of the institutions in Liverpool, such as the Royal Institution, acted as mini-universities. However, University College opened in 1881 with 93 students and 6 professors, including the physicist who later became Sir Oliver Lodge and who took the first clinical 'X-Ray' in Liverpool. The Victoria Building was built in 1889, designed by local architect Alfred Waterhouse, and incorporated a Senate Chamber, large theatre, and the Jubilee Clock Tower. Full University status followed in 1903. Among its more famous tutors can be listed three Nobel Prize Winners: Sir Ronald Ross (linked malaria with the mosquito — Nobel Prize 1902), Sir James Chadwick (a discoverer of the neutron, Nobel Prize 1935) and Sir Charles Sherrington (world famous for his work on the nervous system — Nobel Prize 1932.

Other distinguished names on the teaching staff have included Sir James G. Frazer, professor of Anthropology, 1907-22, and author of 'The Golden Bough'; Sir Charles Reilly and Sir Patrick Abercrombie (Architecture); Jenks (Law); Peet (Egyptology); Sir Bernard Pares (Russian); Gann (Archaeology, 1919-38), Powicke (History) Hilditch (Industrial Chemistry), Hele-Shaw (Engineering) and Gilmour Professors of Spanish, Peers and Fitzmaurice-Kelly, author of "History of Spanish Literature" and "Life of Miguel de Cervantes Saavedra". Sir William Banks, an early advocate for operations for cancer of the breast, was instrumental in improving and organising the medical faculty, and another pioneer in the development of the medical faculty was Reginald Harrison who established street ambulances in Liverpool. Lord Holford and Lord Cohen were two who taught, as well as being taught, at the University.

Two lecturers in Social Science at the University, Tony Lane and Kenneth Roberts produced the first major account of a British industrial dispute with their book "Strike at Pilkingtons", in 1971. An absorbing book, it deals with the industrial action at the St. Helen's glass factory which started on 3 April, 1970.

Hugh Jones was at the University when he won the first London Marathon in 1982. He was second in 1986.

The University has famous Botanical Gardens at Ness, donated by the daughter of the Liverpool cotton broker whose family founded the famous Bees Seeds Ltd. There is a Veterinary Field Section and a marine biology unit in the Isle of Man. The University has over 10,000 students and nearly 1,000 academic staff.

Happy Panto Days.

V

VAUGHAN, Frankie

One of Britain's most popular and enduring entertainers was born Frank Ephraim Abelson in Devon Street, off London Road, Liverpool, 10,000 leg kicks and 4,000 "Hello, Dollies" ago. Rocketed to stardom in the 1950's after his performance in "These Dangerous Years" and went on to appear with Marilyn Monroe in "Lets Make Love". Frank didn't much take to Hollywood and returned to Britain to continue his stage and recording career. Recorded "Green Door" when Shakin' Stevens couldn't even reach the handle. His other smash hits include: "Tower of Strength", "Give Me the Moonlight", "Kisses Sweeter than Wine", etc. His considerable efforts on behalf of Boys' Clubs should qualify him for the lead role in "Sweet Charity" to follow his success on the London stage in "42nd Street". His stage name resulted from his Jewish grandmothers affectionate description of him being her "Number Vone" (No.1).

VAUGHAN, Norman

Became nationally known when he took over from Bruce Forsyth as compère of "Sunday Night at the London Palladium" in 1962, and introduced the catch phrases "swingin" and "dodgy" to the shows' massive audience. Born in Liverpool, at 32 Barry Street, Walton, in 1927.

VERNON, Roy

Stylish, spindle-legged Everton and Welsh international striker of the early 1960's. He skippered the team in their 1963 Championship win, and scored 27 goals during the season including a hat trick in the match that clinched the Title, against Fulham at Goodison.

VERNONS GIRLS

Vocal group who, with alterations in personnel, became The Ladybirds and The Breakaways. Were prominent as backing singers but did achieve minor success with the Scouse flavour of "You Know What I Mean" in 1962. They weren't the only ones to go for the jackpot, however, as the other famous pools firm had a big draw with the Littlewoods Songsters, a much bigger group frequently to be seen on TV in those days.

The Vernons Girls appearing with Michael Holliday in his BBC TV show, "Holliday at Home", in 1963.

VESTEY, William (Lord Vestey)

1859-1940. Founded the Union Cold Storage Company with his brother, Sir Edmund Vestey, sons of Samuel Vestey of Liverpool. Educated at Liverpool Institute, he built a freezing plant in Argentina and created the Blue Star Line. He and his brother were the donors of a Tower at Liverpool Cathedral and donated the 14½ ton Bourdon Bell, named Great George in honour of George V. Created a baron, 1921.

VIOLENT PLAYGROUND

The 1957 film set in Liverpool starring Stanley Baker, John Slater, Anne Heywood, etc., and featuring Freddie Fowell as a young hoodlum. Young Freddie went on to find fame as Freddie Starr.

Williamson Square at an unearthly hour. The former Theatre Royal (Union Cold Storage) prior to redevelopment.

Stanley Baker talks to Bessie Braddock during filming.

113

WACKERSDÖRF
West German nuclear site.

WAKEFIELD, Charles Cheers (Viscount Wakefield)
1859-1941. The well-oiled Liverpudlian! Entrepreneur and philanthropist who founded the lubricating oils company and used as a trade name "Castrol". He was educated at Liverpool Institute and was Lord Mayor of London in 1915. He financed the pioneering flights of Amy Johnson, Alan Cobham and the motor speed trials of Henry Segrave. Chairman of the RAF Benevolent Fund and a great benefactor to hospitals, the British Museum and the British Academy.

WATERHOUSE, Alfred, RA, LLD
1830-1905. Principal architect of his time, born in Liverpool and responsible for Royal Infirmary, Liverpool, Turner Memorial Home, Dingle, North Western Hotel, Liverpool, Manchester Town Hall and Assize Court Building, Caius and Pembroke Colleges, Cambridge, the south front and Hall at Balliol College, Oxford and the Oxford and Cambridge Unions. In London, National Liberal Club, Natural History Museum, City & Guilds Institute, Surveyors Institution Westminster, University College Hospital, Prudential Assurance Building and St. Paul's School.

WATERLOO CUP
The premier coursing event started in 1836 by the proprietor of the Waterloo Hotel, Ranelagh Street, Liverpool, and run at Altcar. The proprietor, William Lynn, was the first winning owner.

WATERLOO R.U.F.C.
Founded in 1882, Waterloo have had many fine teams and produced many international players. The green, red and whites play at Blundellsands and their first international player was H. G. Periton in 1925. He went on to play 21 times for England and was unique in that he was the only Irish-born player to captain England.
Richard Greenwood scored a try on his England debut in 1967 against Ireland in Dublin, and became England captain in 1968/69 as well as leading Lancashire to the County title. He was also responsible for starting England practice sessions prior to international games, at the players' personal expense. Other international players have included: Toft, (an England captain), Rimmer, Bazley, Guest, Sydall and Colin Fisher, who emulated his father when he was chosen as Scotland's hooker. They reached the John Player Final in 1977 and, as well as producing British Lions, had a representative in England teams from 1934 to 1960.

WATERS, Stan
(Now Stan Hughes). Dockers "Restaurant" renowned for traditional Mersey fare. Wet Nellies, Scouse Pies, Flies' Cemeteries (Eccles Cakes), black puddings, chip-and-sauce butties and "dirty big" mugs of tea. In recent times the Dock Road cafeteria's culinary arts have developed but the price is still right . . . "Come On Down". Also renowned for traditional fayre, is **Frank's Café**, on the Dock Road opposite the Waterloo Dock, particularly the enormous breakfasts. Owner Frank Smith's special culinary delights have received an Egon Ronay accolade. It is not known whether the Junior Health Minister has dined there.

WEBSTER, Sir Charles Kingsley
Merchant Taylors educated, and Professor of History at Liverpool University. After serving in the Intelligence Corps, he did the British preparatory work on the formation of the United Nations. Amongst his publications were "Foreign Policy of Palmerston" (2 vols) and "The Congress of Vienna".

WEBSTER, Sir David
1903-1971. A great administrator who was once General Manager at Bon Marché and Lewis's stores in Liverpool. Educated at Holt School, Liverpool, and Oxford University, he was General Administrator at the Royal Opera House Covent Garden from 1946 to 1970, and was Chairman of Liverpool Philharmonic Society and a Director of Southern Television. During his time at Covent Garden he established the Opera House as the permanent home of Sadler's Wells Ballet and both received their Royal Charters during his regime.

WEEKLY BRIDES
Our sympathy to all the Mersey brides-to-be who have been 'duped' by popular Radio City DJ Johnny Kennedy. Born in Anfield he once sang 'Come Back to Sorrento' at the Pavilion, Lodge Lane when he was 12. A former teacher at Forefield Lane school and hit recorder of 'Stay in Your Own Back Yard'.

WELCH, Leslie
The Memory Man. His incredible sports knowledge was severely tested at a packed theatre in Liverpool some years ago. Having invited the audience to test his knowledge he was asked "Who has got a Cup Winner's Medal, an England cricket cap and a Rugby League Championship medal?" After much deliberation and memory-racking the great man had to admit, "No, I'm sorry; you've got me there. Who is it?" The reply was quick, triumphant and reportedly accurate: "The pawnbroker in Lodge Lane". Welch 0-Liverpool 1.

WELLAND, Colin
Actor and playwright who first achieved national recognition playing a policeman in "Z Cars". Born in Liverpool, he left when quite young to go a little further down the East Lancs Road. Presumably the Rugby League on Merseyside wasn't up to standard. He won awards on a regular basis in the early 1970's but his most acclaimed success was for the screenplays for "Yanks" and the Oscar-winning "Chariots of Fire". An archetypical Northerner, he best illustrated the great North/South divide in his play "Say Goodnight to Grandma".

WELLIE
An old Liverpudlian abbreviation for 'Wellington' (as in boot). Now nationally adopted . . . and yet another example of the phenomenal influence the City provides in the cultural life of Britain!

114

WEMBLEY

The Merseyside clubs' second ground, conveniently situated on the north side of London for easier access.

WHITEHEAD, E. A. (Ted)
Merseyside playwright best known for "The Foursome" and "Alpha Beta".

WHITTAKER, Sir Frederick
1893-1968. Liverpool civil engineer responsible for Royal Naval Dockyard, Singapore Naval Base and the Orkney Causeway. Educated at Liverpool Institute and Liverpool University, he was President of the Institute of Engineers and the Admiralty's Civil Engineer-in-Chief (1940-1954). Knighted in 1945 and made Commander, Legion D'Honneur, in 1947.

WHITTY, Dame May
Born in Liverpool in 1865, the daughter of a former Editor of the Daily Post. After a distinguished stage career she was made a Dame Commander in 1918 and in later life settled in Hollywood where she began making films.
She was nominated for an Oscar in 1937 for her performance in "Night Must Fall" and was Hitchcock's vanishing lady in "The Lady Vanishes". She died in 1948.

WILKINSON, Kitty
1786-1860. A window at Liverpool Cathedral is dedicated to the memory of this remarkable woman who nursed the sick, fed the hungry, cared for unwanted children, washed cholera infected clothing, and many other examples of humanitarianism. She herself was from a poor background, with little or no money of her own, and was largely instrumental in providing the worlds' first public wash-house.

WILLIAMS, Allan
First manager of the Beatles. Responsible for their German exposure. Former owner of the Jacaranda and Blue Angel Clubs, scene of the scene in the sixties.

WILLIAMS, Sir Harold Herbert
1886-1964. The Liverpudlian who could have been a Lilliputlian. Educated at Liverpool College, he was a biographer of Swift and leading authority on Gulliver's Travels. Ordained as a priest, called to the Bar (1930), Cambridge University lecturer, President of the Bibliographical Society (1938-44) and Chairman of Hertfordshire County Council. He published several of his own works including "Two Centuries of English Novels" (1911) and "Modern English Writers" (1918).

WILSON, Sir Harold
Huyton MP who became Prime Minister in 1964 and awarded the Beatles their MBEs. A Yorkshireman, it suited him, in his ambitious days, to be mistaken for a Liverpudlian when the city was described as being the 'centre of the universe'. The Pipe and Gannex pub in Knowsley is named after him. He attended Wirral Grammar School and met his future wife Mary at the Tennis Club in Bebington.

WILSON, KEPPEL and BETTY
No, not an old Everton half-back line, but one of Britain's most famous Music Hall acts. The act was together for 56 years and there were seven "Betty's" in all. Their speciality was an eccentric Egyptian sand dance. Jack Wilson was from Liverpool. He died in 1971, eight years after the act performed its last show.

WHERE ARE YOU NOW?

Youngsters from Blessed Margaret Clitherow School at Otterspool in 1973. Can we have a response for next year's edition, please, girls?

WILTON, Robb

"The Day War Broke Out" was the most famous opening line of this great Liverpool comedian of music hall, radio and films. A comedian's comedian of exquisite timing with a gentle droll delivery, the story goes that Wilton learnt his sense of timing from the great George Robey. On one occasion that they met, Wilton told Robey that he had gone to see him when he was a lad in Liverpool. "I didn't think you were very funny but you did have great timing", Wilton told the Prime Minister of Mirth. To which Robey replied "Well, you are very funny and you can time". His much-loved radio show "Mr. Muddlecombe" was broadcast on Thursday nights during the Second World War. He died in 1957, aged 75.

WIZARD'S DEN

Renowned Liverpool 'joke' shop which was located in Moorfields, frequented by many generations of Liverpool schoolboys between 9 and 90.

WOLFSON, Brian

The Liverpudlian appointed Chairman of the British Institute of Management, taking over from Sir Peter Parker in September 1986. He is also Chairman Anglo-Nordic Holdings, the consortium that took over Wembley Stadium. A Liverpool FC follower, on taking up his appointment as Chairman BIM, he was quoted as saying that he thought Britain could learn a lot from Liverpool FC. "There is only one way to play . . . and that is to win". He also believes that Merseyside has the potential to become one of Europe's principal tourist areas.

WOOD, Mrs. John

Famous actress/manager, born in Liverpool in 1831, she went to America to manage the Olympia Theatre in New York. Returning to England she managed the St. James Theatre and the New Royal Court Theatre in London.

WOOLWORTH, Frank Winfield

Surely not a Scouser. No, but he did open his first British store in Church Street, Liverpool in 1909. And indeed he opened his third store in London Road, Liverpool. The Church Street store closed in 1983 as part of the company's rationalisation plans, but you can still see the *original* Woolworth sign on a gable wall in Church Street.

WORLOCK, Most Rev. Derek John Harford

Born 4.2.1920. Archbishop of Liverpool since 1976, previously Bishop of Portsmouth, 1965-1976, and Private Secretary to Archbishop of Westminster from 1945-1964. He was made a Knight Commander of Holy Sepulchre of Jerusalem in 1966. Since arriving in Liverpool has enjoyed a close working relationship with Bishop Sheppard (a sort of the "Saint and Saint" show) and has been particularly vocal in highlighting the needs of the inner city and social deprivation in modern Britain. His efforts have given a positive evangelical lead in Liverpool. His publications include "Take One at Bedtime" (anthology).

WYNDHAM, Sir Charles

Born in Liverpool in 1837, the son of a Liverpool surgeon, became one of the most famous names in Theatre. He served in the American Civil War as a surgeon before becoming an actor. His first performance was with John Wilkes Booth (Lincoln's assassin). In London, he managed the Criterion Theatre before building the theatre that bears his name.

Brian Burgess (centre) joins Arthur Dooley and Alan Williams (at the rear) in a protest outside the Walker Art Gallery in 1969. The three horsemen were protesting that too much "outsiders art" was being exhibited at a John Moores Exhibition.

X

"X"

Placed correctly on the coupons of the famous Liverpool firms of Littlewoods and Vernons, has made poor men rich and kept millions of hopes and dreams alive for decades.

Responsible for heartache, too, the most ill-fated being Viv Nicholson who announced that she was going to "spend, spend, spend" on winning her fortune and whose life thereafter was filled with tragedy and despair.

X-RAY

Liverpool was the first city to organise a mass 'X-Ray' campaign for its citizens, to combat Tuberculosis, etc., in 1959.

Y

YATES, Ivan R.

Born 1929. Appointed Chief Executive British Aerospace, Aircraft Group, 1983. Educated at Liverpool Collegiate and Liverpool University.

YATES, Pauline

Liverpool-born and educated at Childwall Valley High School. Her many TV roles included the long-suffering Mrs. Perrin in "The Rise and Fall of Reginald Perrin", playing opposite fellow Liverpudlian, Leonard Rossiter. Married to actor/writer, Donald Churchill.

YATES, Sir Thomas

Born in Wallasey and educated at St. Mary's School, Wallasey, he was General Secretary, National Union of Seamen, and Chairman of the TUC (1957-58).

YATES' WINE LODGE

Famed hostelries in the city, renowned or notorious for the availability of cheap Australian white wine (nowadays, cheap . . . ish). Many a participant, finding themselves spending the night in the Bridewell to recover from their excesses, has been described as being "in off the white". They retain their popularity for a night of 'atmospheric Liverpudlianism'.

YEAMES, William Frederick

Painter of what is probably the most famous and popular work of art to be seen in the Walker Art Gallery: "And when did you last see your father?"

YELLOW SUBMARINE

Film, song, Garden Festival exhibit and inspired Beatle fantasy. Epic fairytale marinated in sardonic scouse satire and psychedelically packaged by Peter Max. The film broke new ground, the song became a children's classic and the exhibit received a Royal boarding party.

"YESTERDAY"

This Lennon-McCartney classic has been recorded more times than any other song in musical history . . . well over 1,000 versions.

YIP, David

Liverpool-Chinese actor best-known for BBC TV role as "The Chinese Detective".

YOSHIDA, Mr.

A Liverpool Echo obituary "Mr. Yoshida came to Liverpool from Japan . . . although he was a second cousin to the Emperor Hirohito, he was known to nearly all his acquaintances as Paddy Murphy".

"YOSSER" Hughes

Character, brilliantly played by Bernard Hill, in Alan Bleasdale's award-winning BBC drama hit "Boys from the Black Stuff". "Yosser" became a national cult figure who introduced two catchphrases which, in their simple and direct way, reflect ironically contemporary British society: "Gizza job" and "I can do that".

Yosser and that wall.

YOUNG, Alex

A Scotsman who became a Mersey soccer legend. Appropriately signed from that most classic sounding of soccer teams, Heart of Midlothian, he played for Everton in the 1960's with silky skill and style.

His blond ghost-like appearance gave rise to his nickname — 'the Golden Vision' — the title of which was used for a TV play set in Liverpool by Neville Smith and Gordon Honeycombe. Young reserved many of his most majestic performances for Goodison and, after his departure, his 'ghost' remained at the ground, as successive Everton teams tried to recapture the skill and style he epitomised.

YOUNGMAN, Henny

Born in Liverpool, he left as a very young man to become one of America's best-known comedians.

Z

Z-CARS

Trend-setting police drama TV series of the 1960's; it set new standards for realistic documentary/drama, one of the earliest of its genrè. Many of its leading actors became stars: James Ellis, Brian Blessed, Colin Welland, Stratford Johns and the late Leonard Williams, the Liverpudlian actor who played "Sgt. Twentyman" the much admired desk sargeant — ("Get it down in the book, lad!"). The theme tune, "Johnny Todd", became one of TV's best known and was adopted by Everton FC to herald the arrival on the pitch of the home team at Goodison Park. Newtown, the fictional setting, was based on Kirkby, Liverpool.

ZIEGLER, Anne

Liverpool singer who was one half of one of the country's best-known singing duos of the 1940's and 1950's. The other half? ... Webster Booth — The couple married in 1938 and now live at Penrhyn Bay, North Wales.

ZIGGY

The Liverpool character introduced to TV's "Grange Hill" in 1986. Played by George Wilson, chosen after a mammoth audition, Ziggy Greaves has been able to cope successfully with the school's timetable and extra-curricular activities.

I-ZINGARI

Liverpool's best known amateur soccer league. "I, Zingari" is Italian and means "The Gypsies" or "The Wanderers". For many years the clash between Aigburth People's Hall and Florence Albion was the "Match of the Season".

With the emergence of Sunday football, Merseyside soon developed the biggest amateur Sunday football scene in Europe, with full-time being appropriately timed to ensure revitalisation before closing time.

"Imagine ALL the people . . ."

John Lennon,
1940-1980

'There are places I'll remember . . .

ILLUSTRATIONS

READERS RESPONSE

There are, obviously, omissions in this anthology. Do you think there is a significant omission? A personality? An event? If so, please write and tell us about it. WHITBREAD will give a Party to the winners in 1987. Further details will be announced in the Liverpool Echo . Please write to:

Whitbread Book of Scouseology,
c/o Liverpool Echo,
P. O. Box 48,
Old Hall Street,
Liverpool L69 3ER.

The authors and the publishers wish to thank all the photographers and their agencies, especially the Liverpool Echo, who gave their permission for their work to be included in this book. Our thanks also to those we were unable to trace or contact.

Whilst every care has been taken in the compilation of this anthology, and the statements contained herein are believed to be correct at the time of publication, the publishers, authors and sponsors shall not be liable for any inaccuracies.

ANSWERS

CROSSWORD:

ACROSS

1 & 2. LOL COTTERELL. The bakery van driver who delivered to Anfield and via Esther Rantzen's show, "That's Life", found himself in Tommy Smith's benefit match.

3. DELMONTS, Freddie Starr's former backing group.

4. HACKETT, Johnny, who's a 'dead ringer' for the French clown.

5 & 6. GERRY BYRNE. One 'Gerry' who didn't bomb our chippy unfortunately broke a collar bone in the 1965 Liverpool v Leeds Utd. FA Cup Final and played the full match (in pre-substitute days).

7. HOLLY Johnson who put so much energy into relaxing.

8. WYNNE, Arthur, inventor of this tormenting device.

9. MELBA, Paul, star of stage, screen and ice-cream parlour.

11. ITMA. Tommy Handley's acronym-titled radio show.

22. OMD. Did you experience the 'initial' success that they had?

26 & 27. TOMMY LAWRENCE. The fans' affectionate nickname for Liverpool's keeper of the 60's.

DOWN

10. FOURMOST. They arrived too late to call themselves a 'quartet'.

11. TEARDROP Explodes, current Liverpool Group

12. TIGER, Dick, Liverpool-based boxer of Nigerian origin who died in New York.
The Chinese Year of the Tiger began in February, 1986.

13. RATTLES. German rock group that signified Hamburg's token response to Liverpool band invasions of the early 60's by visiting the Cavern to capture hearts and ears.

14. SANDON, Johnny — original lead singer of the Searchers, he left when the group went to Hamburg and joined the Remo Four.

15 & 16. WET NELLY. Traditional Liverpool cake of syrup-impregnated pastry.

17. QUICKLY, Tommy, early starter in the Liverpool music scene of the 60's. Consistent with his name, was an early finisher as well.

18, 19 & 20. BLACK AND TAN. Guinness and Mild

23. EGREMONT. An anagram of the name of a ferryboat and a district on the Wirral.

24. GOREE. Piazzas. Dock Road location with slave connections.

25. CANNING Place. According to the scouse sea shanty, Maggie May's favourite beat.

QUIZ:

1 King John. 2 Sudley Art Gallery, Aigburth. 3 Pig and Whistle, Chapel Street. 4 Start of Radio City. 5 Jimmy Nicoll. 6 Eph Longworth. 7 William Roscoe. 8 The Brothers McGregor. 9 Sefton Park. 10 Lewis's. 11 Shakespeare Theatre. 12 OMD. 13 Valentine's Brook. 14 Limekiln Lane. 15 Brownlow Hill. 16 W C Cuff. 17 Wayne Bickerton. 18 Royal Tan — National Winners 1948-1954. 19 Herbert Rowse. 20 Alan Rudkin. 21 Gabriel, Brian Harris, Harvey. 22 Kevin Keegan for Hamburg v. Liverpool — Super Cup Liverpool won 6-0. 23 i) 1807 ii)1835 iii) 18 December, 1865 (13th Amendment to Constitution). 24 Merseyside female wrestler. 25 Rory Storm. 26 Pat Cooke. 27 Walter Weller. 28 1967 — 22 November. 29 Archbishop Richard Downey. 30 Humphrey Brooke.

Tiebreaker Answer:

Liverpool's first radio station which started broadcasting in June 1924, from a studio above Cottle's Edinburgh Cafe in Lord Street (it closed in July 1931). "Auntie" Muriel was Muriel Levy from Allerton, Liverpool. Well known Childrens Hour broadcaster.

QUEUE PICTURE QUIZ:

1 Alarm clocks etc., from Wilkins Shop
2 Blankets, rubber boots and ex WRNS skirts from the Army and Navy store
3 Sweets
4 Tickets for Everton cup game at Sheffield Wednesday
5 C & A Modes January Sale. The queue was headed for the second year running by Mrs Ellen Ramejkiss of Vauxhall Road
6 The 'chara' to Blackpool
7 Coke from Athol Street gas works
8 The Isle of Man boat
9 A House to Let in Ono Street, Wavertree being negotiated by Boult, Son and Maples
10 Smallpox vaccinations in Hatton Garden